By The Editors of Consumer Guide®

Electrical Repairs Made Easy

Contents

HOW IT WORKS **4**
Although electricity and electrical theory can be a difficult subject to learn in depth, practical electricity as it applies to residential wiring is neither difficult to understand nor hard to work with.

How Your Home Is Wired **5**

The Service Equipment **6**

Overload Protection **7**

Branch and Feeder Circuits **9**

Wire Types and Capacities **11**

Electrical Safety **13**

Electrical Grounding **16**

Electrical Codes **17**

REPAIRING AND REPLACING ELECTRICAL COMPONENTS **18**
Professional service isn't cheap. Why not perform many simple repairs yourself? Often, replacements and repairs only require those tools you are likely to have around the house. However, just be sure you make safety your first priority.

Tools **19**

Restoring a Circuit **21**

Coping with a Power Outage **22**

Checking Outlet Polarity **23**

Louis Weber, President
Publications International, Ltd.
3841 West Oakton Street
Skokie, Illinois 60076

Permission is never granted for commercial purposes.

Printed and bound by Graficki Zavod Hrvatske & Printing House Founded 1874

3   4   5   6   7   8   9   10

Library of Congress Catalog Card Number: 79-57309
ISBN: 0-517-301881

Cover Design: Frank E. Peiler
Cover Photography: Dave Jordano Photography Inc.
Illustrations: C. A. Moberg
Acknowledgment: The Editors of Consumer Guide® wish to thank Sears, Roebuck & Co. for allowing us to photograph some of their products.

Rewiring a Lamp **24**

Replacing Appliance Cords **26**

Wall and Ceiling Fixtures **28**

Replacing a Wall Switch **35**

Changing a Broken Receptacle **39**

Repairing a Broken Doorbell **40**

NEW INSTALLATIONS **45**

Installing new fixtures is a bit more complicated than merely fixing the breakdowns in your electrical system or replacing worn-out components, but it is not beyond the scope of safety-conscious do-it-yourselfers.

New Lighting Fixtures **45**

Outdoor Lighting **51**

Installing New Types of Switches **53**

Installing Additional Receptacles **62**

Adding a Branch Circuit **70**

Adding a Ground Fault Interrupter **71**

SPECIAL WIRING INSTALLATIONS **73**

The limit of what you can do with your home's electrical system isn't confined to installing new lamps, fixtures, and circuits. There are a number of special wiring installations that can make your home a more distinctive, attractive, and convenient place in which to live.

Installing a Home Security System **73**

Installing a Home Intercom System **78**

Garage Door Opener **80**

Wiring Your Home for Sound **85**

Built-In Appliances **88**

GLOSSARY **93**

How It Works

Nothing seems to draw the line between primitive and advanced living conditions quite so clearly as the possession of electrically powered devices such as lamps, appliances, and home entertainment systems. We depend on the thin cables that wind through our homes for more than just running luxury and convenience items; we look to our electric system for the high standard of living to which we have become accustomed.

Despite our dependence on electricity, many of us would be hard pressed to explain just how our home power systems work. We plug appliances into receptacles, flip switches, adjust dials, slide levers — and do all of this without a moment's thought as to how what we do relates to how an electrical system actually functions. And furthermore, we would be totally confounded — most of us, that is — if we were to try to fix some component that refuses to perform as it should.

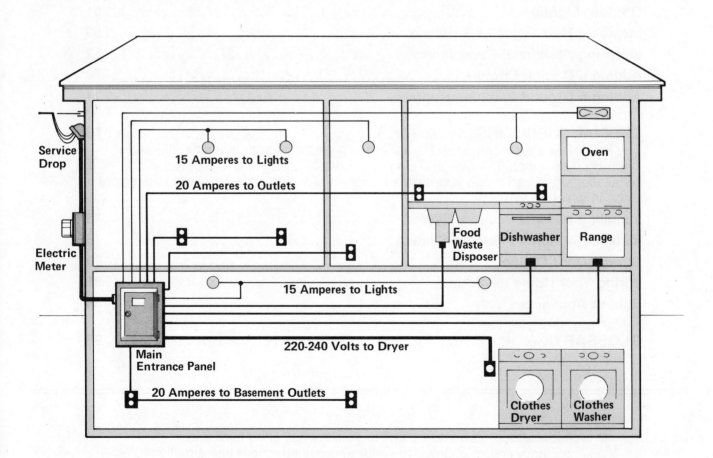

Newer homes have three incoming power lines that supply 110-120/220-240 volts AC. This provides 110-120 volts for lighting, receptacles, and small appliances, as well as 220-240 volts for heavier appliances.

This is a shameful situation. Although electricity and electrical theory can be a difficult subject to learn in depth, practical electricity as it applies to a residential wiring system is neither difficult to understand nor hard to work with. Indeed, there are plenty of good reasons for learning how your home's electrical system works, how you can fix it, and how you can improve its usefulness. You can save yourself a great deal of money by making your own repairs and new installations. In addition, your family's safety could well depend on your knowledge.

HOW YOUR HOME IS WIRED

On the surface, your home's plumbing and electrical systems may seem as different as any two things could be. Yet, there are significant parallels. Water enters your house under pressure (hydraulic pressure, measured in pounds per square inch) through a pipe, and when you turn on a tap, the water flows at a certain rate (gallons per minute). Electricity enters your home through copper (or aluminum, and sometimes both) wires, also under pressure (electrical, called electromotive force or voltage, measured in volts). When you activate an electrical device, the electricity flows at a certain rate (current, measured in amperes). But unlike water, electricity is meant to do work and is converted from energy to power, which is measured in watts. Since household electrical consumption is relatively high, the unit of measure most often used is the kilowatt — or 1,000 watts. The total amount of electrical energy that you consume for any given period is measured by a meter in terms of kilowatt-hours(kwh).

Before we trace your home's electrical system any further, the electric meter deserves further consideration. This is the instrument that records how much electricity you consume. It also helps determine how much you must pay when your electric bill arrives.

| 10,000 | 1,000 | 100 | 10 | Units |

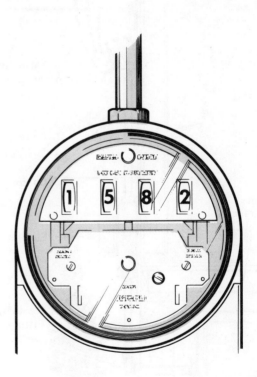

There are two types of electric meters in general use. One displays a series of dials that register the number of kilowatt-hours; the other has slots in which numerals appear, much like a car's odometer.

There are two types of electric meters in general use. One type displays on its face a row of small dials with individual indicators. Each dial registers a certain number of kilowatt-hours of electrical energy. For example, if you were to leave a 100-watt bulb burning for 10 hours, the meter would register 1 kilowatt-hour (10 x 100 = 1000 watt-hours, or 1 kwh). The meter dial at the far right is the one that counts individual kilowatt hours from 1 to 10; the next one to the left counts the electricity consumed from 10 to 100 kilowatt-hours; the third counts up to 1,000, the fourth counts up to 10,000, and the dial at the extreme left counts kilowatt-hours up to 100,000. This type of meter is read from right to left; pay close attention to whether the dials run clockwise or counterclockwise.

The second type of electric meter performs the same function, but instead of individual dials, numerals appear in slots on the meter face, much like the odometer in your car. This meter is read from left to right, and the numbers indicate total electrical consumption. Some meters also use a multiplying factor — the number that appears must be multiplied by 10, for instance, for a true figure in kilowatt-hours. Once you know how to read your meter, you can verify the charges on your electric bill and — perhaps — become a better watchdog of electrical energy consumption and conservation in your home.

The electrical service drop, or supply line, and the meter are as far as the local utility company is involved in your home's electrical system. From that point on, the system is the homeowner's responsibility. The electricity passes from the meter to the service equipment by means of three lines (older houses may have two) that supply 110-120/220-240 volts AC (alternating current). The exact voltage varies, depending on several external factors. This three-wire system allows you to have 110-120 volts for lighting, receptacles, and small appliances, as well as 220-240 volts for an electric range, clothes dryer, water heater and, in some homes, electric heating.

THE SERVICE EQUIPMENT

Electricity enters your home through the service equipment. By strict definition, the service equipment is simply a disconnect device that is mounted in a suitable approved enclosure. Its purpose is to disconnect the service from the interior wiring system. This disconnect might be a set of pull-out fuses, a circuit breaker or, in a few instances, a large switch. The device is usually called a main fuse, main breaker or main disconnect, and often simply "the main." It can be in a separate enclosure, and though it is usually installed inside the building, it can be mounted outdoors in a weatherproof box.

In practice, however, main disconnects are nearly always located inside the house in the top part of a large enclosure that also contains the fuses or circuit breakers, which handle the distribution of power throughout the house. This is called a main entrance panel, main box or entrance box. The three wires from the meter enter this box; and two of them — the heavily insulated black and white lines — are secured in lugs to the tops of a parallel pair of exposed heavy copper bars, called busses, that are positioned vertically toward the center of the box. These two lines are the "live" or "hot" wires. The third wire, generally bare, is the neutral. It is attached to a separate grounding bar or bus — a silver-colored strip usually found at the

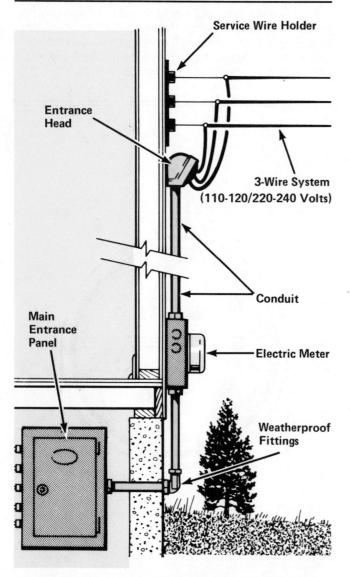

The electrical service drop, or supply line, and the meter are as far as the local utility company is involved in your home's electrical system. From that point on, the system is the homeowner's responsibility.

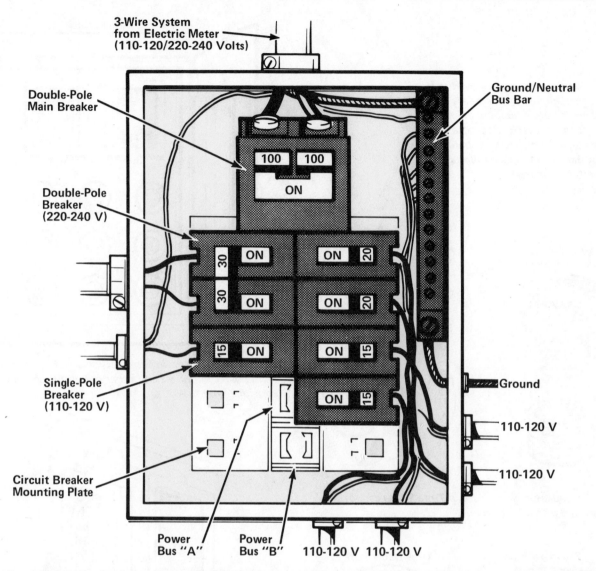

3-Wire System from Electric Meter (110-120/220-240 Volts)

Double-Pole Main Breaker

Double-Pole Breaker (220-240 V)

Single-Pole Breaker (110-120 V)

Circuit Breaker Mounting Plate

Ground/Neutral Bus Bar

100 100
ON

30 ON   ON 20
30 ON   ON 20
15 ON   ON 15
          ON 15

Ground

110-120 V

110-120 V

Power Bus "A"   **Power Bus "B"**   110-120 V   110-120 V

A main disconnect is nearly always located inside the house in the top part of a large enclosure also containing the fuses or circuit breakers. This is the main entrance panel, main box or entrance box. It distributes electricity to various circuits.

bottom or to one side of the main box. In most homes this ground bus is actually connected to the ground — the earth — by a heavy solid copper wire that is clamped to a cold water pipe or to an underground bar or plate.

OVERLOAD PROTECTION

Power is distributed through your house by means of various electrical circuits that originate in the main entrance panel. The 110-120-volt circuits have two conductors — one neutral (white) wire and one "hot" (black) wire. Occasionally, three conductors may be used inside one jacket to serve as two circuits, with one

red (hot) wire, one black (hot) wire, and a common neutral or white wire. The 220-240-volt circuits may consist of two hot wires alone, or a third, neutral wire may be added. In all cases, the "hot" lines are attached to fuses or circuit breakers, which, in turn, are attached directly to the "hot" main busses. The neutral wire is always connected to the ground bus, and *never* under any circumstances passes through a fuse or circuit breaker.

Fuses and circuit breakers are safety devices built into your electrical system. Since the typical homeowner probably does not know about wire current-carrying capacity, the fuses or circuit breakers are there to prevent overloading of a particular circuit.

To protect against serious overloads, fuses—and circuit breakers—are designed to blow—or trip—stopping the flow of current to the overloaded cable. For example, a 15-ampere fuse should blow when the current passing through it exceeds 15 amperes.

Fuse Panel

In addition to screw-in fuses, a typical main fuse panel has a main disconnect and other pull-out blocks with cartridge-type fuses.

Type S Fuse and Adapter

Remove by Turning Counterclockwise

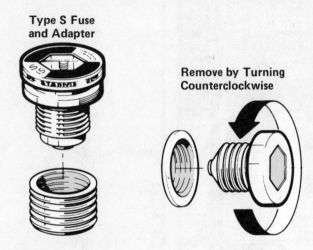

Unless an adapter base is used, a Type S fuse cannot be inserted into a fuse panel.

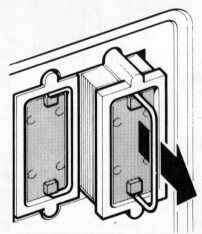

To reach the cartridge fuses, you simply pull the blocks out of the main entrance panel.

Standard Fuse   **Time-Delay Fuse**

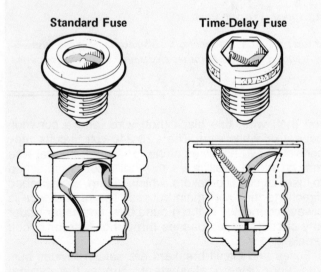

The standard fuse and time-delay fuse are other common types used. The latter does not blow if the current overload is only a momentary surge.

Cartridge Fuses

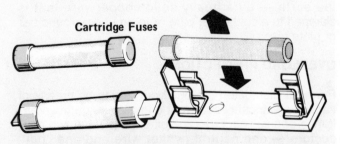

Cartridge fuses, which can be checked with a continuity tester, are held in place by spring clips.

Were they not present and you were to operate too many appliances on a single circuit, the cable would get extremely hot, short circuit, and quite possibly start a fire.

To prevent electrical overloads, fuses and circuit breakers are designed to blow or trip, stopping the flow of current to the overloaded cable. For example, a 15-ampere fuse should blow when the current through it exceeds 15 amperes, and a 20-ampere circuit breaker should trip when the current through it exceeds 20 amperes. A fuse that blows or a circuit breaker that trips is not faulty; it is doing its job properly, indicating that there is trouble somewhere in the circuit. Either there are too many appliances plugged in, or some malfunctioning device — like an appliance with an internal short — is connected to the circuit.

A blown fuse or a tripped circuit breaker is the signal to look for trouble. It makes no sense to replace a blown fuse or to reset a tripped circuit breaker until you have located and eliminated the cause of the trouble. **Caution:** Never try to defeat this built-in safety system by replacing a fuse with one of a larger current-carrying capacity. The fuse or circuit breaker capacity should equal, or be less than, the current-carrying capacity, or ampacity, of the conductors. The older Edison-base type of plug fuses can be interchanged in certain sizes, as can some cartridge fuses. But if you were to replace a 15-ampere fuse with a 25-ampere version, you could be placing yourself in a highly dangerous situation. Placing a copper penny behind a blown fuse is likewise sure to lead to disaster. Certain types of circuit breakers can also be interchanged, but as with fuses, they *never* should be. The newer Type S fuses are not interchangeable, for safety's sake.

BRANCH AND FEEDER CIRCUITS

From the fuses or circuit breakers, circuits go to all the devices in your home that require electrical power. There are two types of circuits: branch and feeder. Feeder circuits, which are not found in every house, are relatively heavy cables that travel from the main entrance panel to other, smaller distribution panels. Called subpanels or load centers, they are located in remote parts of the house or in outbuildings. These auxiliary panels are used for redistribution of "bulk" power, such as in a garage or workshop.

All of the circuits that run from either the main entrance panel or other, smaller panels to the various points of use are branch circuits. For 110-120-volt needs, a circuit branches out through a circuit breaker from one of the main busses and from the ground bus. For 220-240 volts, many circuits use only the two main busses. But, all three wires are needed for devices that operate on both 110-120 and 220-240 volts, such as an electric range, and for the 220-240-volt appliances that require the third wire for a neutral.

Circuit Breaker Panel

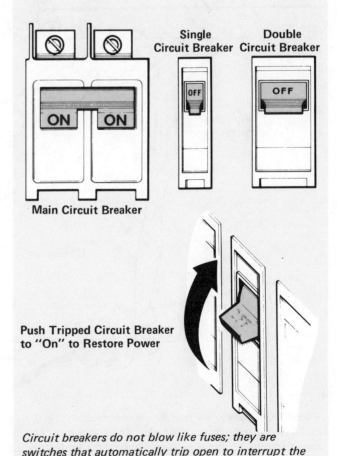

Single Circuit Breaker

Double Circuit Breaker

Main Circuit Breaker

Push Tripped Circuit Breaker to "On" to Restore Power

Circuit breakers do not blow like fuses; they are switches that automatically trip open to interrupt the flow of electrical current when it overloads the circuit.

The 110-120-volt branch circuits go through fuses or circuit breakers, which are labeled either 15 amperes or 20 amperes. The 15-ampere branches go to ceiling lamps and wall receptacles in rooms where less energy-demanding devices, such as floor and table lamps, are found. The larger 20-ampere branch circuits go to receptacles in the kitchen, dining, and laundry areas — anywhere that heavy-duty appliances like washing machines, dryers, dishwashers, refrigerators, and toasters are used. Every home should have at least two 20-ampere circuits.

A 15-ampere circuit can handle a total of 1,800 watts and a 20-ampere circuit a total of 2,400 watts; but these figures represent circuits that are fully loaded. It is a good practice to limit the load on a 15-ampere

circuit to no more than 1,440 watts, and not exceed 1,920 watts on a 20-ampere line. Add up the individual wattages for all lamps and appliances plugged into each circuit to make sure that there is no overload anywhere in your home.

When computing the load on each branch circuit, be sure to allow for the fact that many motor-driven appliances draw more current when the motor is just starting up than when running. A refrigerator, for example, might draw up to 15 amperes initially, but settle down to around 4 amperes quickly. Suppose that the refrigerator is plugged into a 20-ampere branch circuit and that a 1,000-watt electric toaster — which draws a little more than 8 amperes — is also plugged into that circuit. If the refrigerator motor starts while the toaster

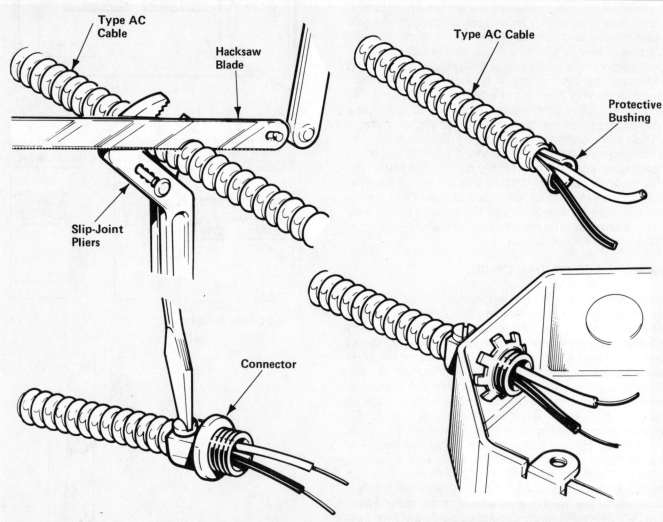

Some local codes may specify metal-clad cable--Type AC--for some applications. AC cable, however, requires some different installation procedures. The armor must be cut at a 45° angle and slid off the wires (top, left). A bushing is used to protect the wires (top, right). Finally, to connect the cable, a connector is clamped to the end of the armor (bottom, left) and then to an electrical box with a connector nut (bottom, right).

is toasting, the total current load exceeds the current-carrying capacity of the circuit, and the fuse blows or the circuit breaker trips.

WIRE TYPES AND CAPACITIES

Several types of wires have been used over the years to run residential electrical circuits. Some older homes may still have circuits wired with the knob-and-tube system, which employs separated individual conductors, surface-mounted and running on or through porcelain insulators. Such wiring should be replaced.

There are numerous types of cables used in modern wiring systems, and each is designed for particular purposes. In residential applications, however, there are only three types that are widely used in wiring branch circuits. One is the metal-clad Type AC cable, which is installed wherever local electrical codes specify that the cables must be metal-clad. Type NM cable is by far the most commonly used type; it is a plastic-sheathed cable. Unless local codes specify otherwise, this is the cable to choose for all indoor, dry-location residential wiring, except for certain kinds of appliance circuits that may require other, special types. The somewhat similar Type UF replaces Type NM cable where the circuit must be buried underground or located in wet or corrosive spots; it *cannot,* however, be exposed to sunlight. Most home electricians will find need only for Type NM cable, two- or three-wire in conductor sizes #14 and #12 — perhaps

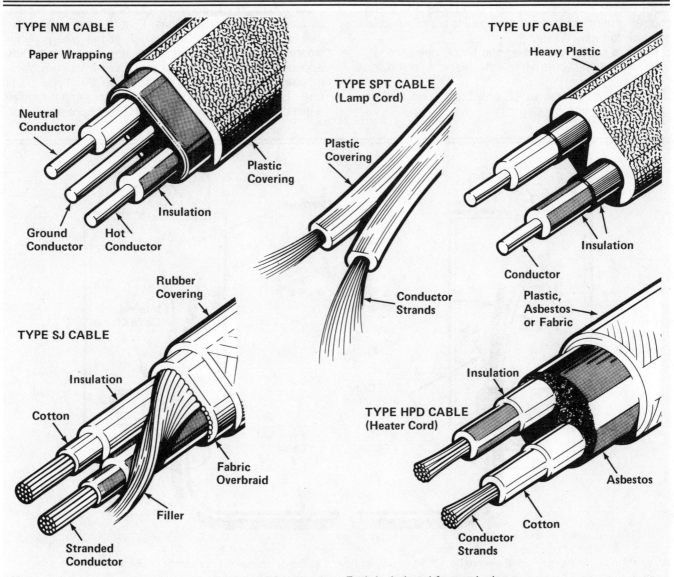

Numerous types of cables are used in modern wiring systems. Each is designed for particular purposes.

occasionally #10 — all with a ground wire (an extra bare conductor). The size of an electrical conductor is determined by its diameter in mils (or thousandths of an inch) measured at 68°F. In this country, that size is translated into trade sizes expressed as gauge numbers that follow the American Wire Gauge (AWG) system. For wiring outdoor lighting circuits and receptacles, and running buried branch circuits, use Type UF in the same sizes; both types are handled in much the same way. A few circuits, such as a range hookup, might require Type SE or some other kind of cable; check the specific requirements with your electrical inspector, electrical supplies dealer, or in applicable electrical codes.

Type NM cable is found inside the walls of nearly all recently constructed homes. It has a tough outer sheath (usually made of plastic), which covers two or more plastic-insulated copper conductors and a bare copper grounding conductor. The insulated wires are color-coded as follows:

- 2-wire cable: one white, one black, one bare.
- 3-wire cable: one white, one black, one red, one bare.
- 4-wire cable: one white, one black, one red, one blue, and one bare.

Type NM cable can be run free through spaces in floors, ceilings or walls. Or, it can be fastened to the sides of exposed joists and studs, secured at least every 4½ feet with approved electrical staples, and also at a point no more than 12 inches from the entrance point into any electrical box. Type NM can also be run through holes bored in structural members, spaced at least 2 inches up from the outside edge, or centered in 2x4's. Staples used to secure the cable should not compress the outer jacket of the cable; corner bends should be gentle and no less than a radius of about 3 inches. The cable must be clamped in place within any electrical box with a minimum 6 inches of free conductor left within the box. The cable also must be a continuous, unbroken run from box to box; a splice or connection can only be made within a box — never out in the open.

As you might expect, one type of wire cannot handle all electrical wiring situations. Fixtures and appliances call for other kinds of wire. Look at the wire on your washing machine, refrigerator or any other heavy-duty appliance and most likely you will see a tough rubber- or plastic-sheathed cord called Type SJ. Type SJ is one of the workhorse cords for appliances that require a great deal of current, but which do not produce heat.

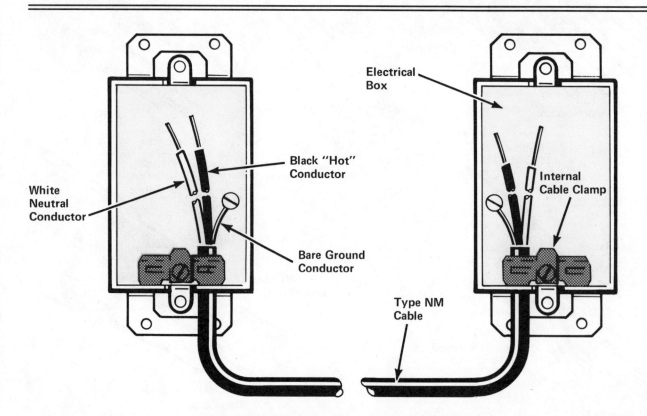

All cable must be a continuous, unbroken run from box to box; a splice or connection can only be made within a box-- never in the open. And, a cable end must be clamped in place within any electrical box.

If you need a heater cord, you can choose between Type HPD and Type HPN. For many years, the cloth-covered HPD — with a packing of asbestos around its inner conductors — monopolized heating cords. With the development of temperature-resistant thermoplastics, however, Type HPN (which looks like heavy lamp cord) is replacing Type HPD on many heat-producing appliances.

The most common lamp cord — also used on radios, television sets, electric clocks, and so forth — is called Type SPT. Each plastic-insulated conductor is composed of many individual strands; that is what makes lamp cord so flexible. Since Type SPT features a molded groove between the two wires for easy splitting, it is often referred to as "zip cord."

Wire that is used properly — that is, only for the purpose for which it was designed and not loaded beyond its capacity — should last the lifetime of a high-quality home or other structure, except for some fixture wires. You must not, however, exceed a particular wire's current-carrying capacity. All wire is rated for capacity; #14 Type NM, for example, has an allowable current-carrying capacity of 15 amperes.

What would happen if you were to load wire beyond its capacity? An occasional quick excess load would probably do no damage whatsoever — except perhaps to blow a fuse or trip a circuit breaker. The wire would not evaporate, disintegrate or suffer some other sort of immediate damage. Over the long term, however, wire that continuously carries excessive current will incur degradation of the copper and the insulation will dry out, flake or crack long before it has served its useful life. A wire's capacity, therefore, refers to the amount of current it can conduct continuously — day in and day out — without suffering any damage.

ELECTRICAL SAFETY

It is the insulation around a conductor that protects you from danger. An electric shock is always distressing, always hazardous, and often fatal. The idea behind electrical safety is that you must avoid physical contact with any live or "hot" part of the circuit. All electrical devices and electrical wiring are designed to provide the greatest measure of safety, but you can defeat any built-in safeguards through carelessness and ignorance. You must understand both the hazards and the precautions those hazards require you to practice if you are to work safely with electricity.

Never do anything that would compromise the integrity of the conductor insulation. Do not, for example, staple an extension cord to a baseboard or to a wall (an illegal practice). The staple can cut through the insulation and create a short circuit, which, in turn, can start a fire. Moreover, you should examine regularly all wiring and discard any cord that has brittle insulation. Replace old cord with new cord that has good insulation.

There is one wire in the electrical system that you can theoretically touch without fear of getting shocked (*if* the circuit is correctly connected), and that is the neutral wire. The problem is, though, that you cannot be certain without testing as to which wire is the neutral, or whether a polarity reversal might have taken place somewhere in the circuit. The equipment grounding circuit, present only in later wiring systems, should also be dead, but there is always the possibility that it might not be properly installed. Nor are identifying marks or colors on the wires always reliable. Therefore, make it a practice to avoid any kind of contact whatsoever with *any* part of a live circuit. This is particularly true when working with poorly done or jury-rigged systems, and with an old type of wiring like BX armored cable. The latter can be particularly hazardous, since the casing itself may well be "hot." Even if the circuit that is to be worked on has been disconnected or turned off, the casing may *still* be hot because of feedback, so check carefully with a circuit tester or voltmeter before starting work.

If you plan to work on a portable electrical device, unplug it; and if you want to work with a household circuit, remove the fuse or trip the circuit breaker to its "off" position. These two safety rules seem almost too obvious to mention, but many people forget to obey them and wind up as casualties of their do-it-yourself electrical repairs.

About the only thing you can do relatively safely with a portable electrical device without first unplugging it is to change a light bulb. *Never* attempt an appliance repair until you disconnect the power cord from the circuit. Do all appliance work with the unit "cold," and do not plug it in again until all your work is finished. Then, if it blows a fuse, disconnect the appliance immediately

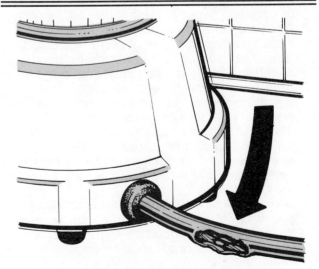

For safety, examine wiring regularly. Replace cords that have brittle or damaged insulation.

HOW DANGEROUS IS ELECTRICITY?

How much electricity is dangerous? For comparison, normal average household voltage is about 115 or 230 volts, alternating at 60 cycles per second. A standard 100-watt bulb draws a little less than 1 ampere of current, a toaster about 7 amperes. A doorbell operates on about 10-12 volts. In tests, some people were found to stand no more than 7/1000 of 1 ampere at 12 volts AC before having to let go of test leads. Others were able to withstand anywhere from 20 to 40 volts at the same current with leads held in dry hands, but lost voluntary control of arm muscles after only a few seconds. Some with thicker-skinned, calloused dry hands could stand momentary jolts of up to 120 volts, but within seconds the current broke down the skin, caused blisters, and greatly increased conductivity.

Shock sensation occurs at as little as 1/1000 of 1 ampere, and 7 to 8 milliamperes causes severe discomfort. If conditions are right, a current of only 30 milliamperes can be fatal!

When a person receives an electrical shock, two things can happen. One, current interferes with the nerves of the breathing control center at the back of the neck, respiration ceases, and artificial respiration must be started immediately; the nerves may or may not recover. Or, current may stop the heart completely or cause it to fibrillate; the heart may or may not recover. So, take all possible precautions and proceed with care and thought when working with electricity. In the interest of electrical safety, follow these precautions:

1. *Before working on any electrical circuit or apparatus, deenergize the circuit by removing plug fuses or tripping a circuit breaker to the "off" position.*
2. *When deenergizing a circuit, remove a plug fuse entirely and put it in your pocket or toolbox, or securely tape a circuit breaker handle in the "off" position. This will prevent the circuit from being turned back on by someone else. In both cases, post a sign at the main entrance panel telling everyone that electrical work is in progress.*
3. *Always assume that an electrical outlet or apparatus is energized until you prove otherwise with a circuit tester or by pulling a disconnect plug. Deenergizing the wrong circuit is easy to do, with unhappy results.*
4. *Do not work on a switched outlet or lighting fixture, even though the switch is turned off, without first deenergizing the circuit. In many switching systems, parts of the circuit are still energized when the switch is off.*
5. *When working in a main entrance panel, always trip the main circuit breaker to the "off" position or re-move the main fuses before removing the panel cover. If possible, cover the top main line connecting lugs, which remain energized, with a piece of corrugated cardboard (a good insulator) wedged into the panel box, to prevent accidental contact.*
6. *When working in a main entrance panel located over a dirt or concrete surface, or any other surface that might be damp, always lay down a scrap of plywood or plank to stand on to isolate yourself from ground.*
7. *When working in a load center or subpanel, always deenergize the entire panel by tripping the appropriate circuit breaker in the main entrance panel to the "off" position or by removing the appropriate fuses.*
8. *Always use tools with insulating handles — wood- or plastic-handled screwdrivers, diagonal cutters with plastic grips, etc.*
9. *In making electrical repairs or installations, always follow safe, accepted practices, procedures, and techniques, and employ proper, approved materials and devices. Never overload circuits, make open splices or connections, mount inaccessible junction boxes, compromise the integrity of conductor insulation, employ improper materials or equipment, or otherwise occasion a potentially hazardous situation. Ignorance is no excuse; make sure that you know what you are doing and why, when working with electricity. You might not get a second chance.*

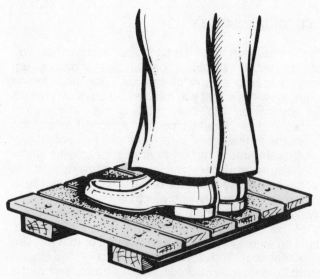

When working in the main panel located over a surface that might be wet or damp, always use a piece of plywood or a wooden platform to isolate yourself from ground.

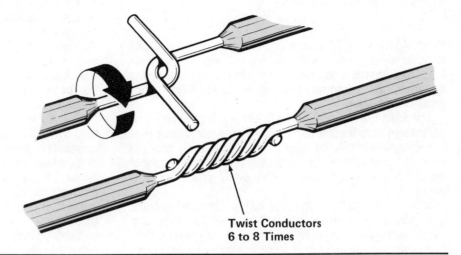

One way to form a wire joint is to twist the ends of conductors together six to eight times. The joint can then be soldered and wrapped with electrical tape.

Twist Conductors
6 to 8 Times

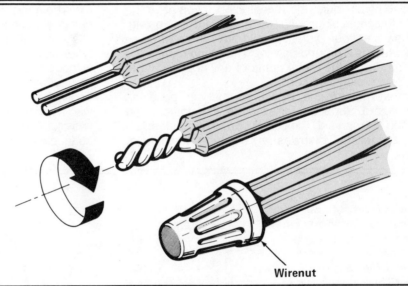

One of the most popular ways to join wires is to use solderless connectors called wirenuts. The conductor ends are twisted together and the wirenut is screwed onto the twisted ends. Make sure, however, that the conductors' insulation goes all the way up to the wirenut and that no bare conductor is exposed.

Wirenut

and do not plug it in until you locate and eliminate the cause of the trouble.

When you change a receptacle or a switch — or do any other work on a circuit — always disconnect the power first. If your system operates with fuses, remove the fuse for the circuit you are working on, and slip the fuse in your pocket or toolbox. Were you to leave it nearby, there always is a chance that someone might put the fuse back in while you are working on the circuit. If your home's electrical system uses circuit breakers, trip the appropriate circuit breaker to its "off" position. Then, to make sure that no one accidentally flips the circuit breaker back on while you are making electrical repairs, put a piece of tape — and a sign telling people what you are doing — over the circuit breaker's handle. The sign, of course, is a good idea for a fuse box as well.

What do you use for light once you deenergize the circuit on which you plan to work? If deenergizing the circuit plunges the area into darkness, use a flashlight — a portable fluorescent lantern works very well — or a trouble light with a long cord that you can plug into a circuit that is still energized.

When you work on an electrical circuit, you must — for safety's sake — make all wire joints and connections inside an approved electrical box. There are several ways to join wires, but the best way is to use solderless connectors of either the crimp-on or screw-on (wirenut) kind. Never connect wires together in a behind-the-wall or in-the-ceiling location that is not accessible to you merely by opening an electrical box. In addition, when joining insulated wires to one another or when fastening them under terminal screws, make sure that no uninsulated (bare) wire extends beyond the connection. Fully insulated wires should go right up to the solderless connector or to the terminal screw.

ELECTRICAL GROUNDING

Proper grounding of your electrical system is essential to your safety. Electricity always follows the path of least resistance, and that path could be *you* whenever an appliance or another electrical component is not grounded.

The idea behind grounding is simply to direct electrical energy into the earth by providing a conductor that is less resistant than you are. This is frequently accomplished by attaching one end of a wire to the frame of an appliance and fastening the other end to a cold water pipe.

Most nonmetallic sheathed cable contains a bare wire that carries the grounded connection to every electrical box, outlet, and appliance in your home. You can usually tell whether your electrical system is grounded by checking the receptacles. If you have the kind that accepts plugs with two blades and one prong, you know that your system should have three wires — one of which is a grounding wire. The prong carries the safety ground to the metal frame of any appliance that has a 3-wire plug and cord.

It is that metal frame, of course, that can pose the safety hazard. Suppose, for example, that some of the insulation surrounding the power cord of a major appliance (refrigerator, dishwasher, washing machine or

clothes dryer) were to wear away just at the point where the cord enters the frame. The contact between the current conductor and the metal frame could make that whole appliance alive with electricity and threaten your safety. In fact, were you to touch the charged metal frame while simultaneously touching a water faucet or a radiator, the current would surge through you and endanger your life.

There are other places throughout the electrical system where conductor/metal contact is a distinct possibility. Wherever wires enter a metal pipe (conduit), where the cord enters a lamp or lamp socket, and where in-wall cable enters an electrical box are a few examples. Surfaces at these points must be free of burrs that could chafe the wire and damage its insulation. Washers, grommets, and special fittings have been devised to protect wire at these various points of entry, but the best thing you can do is to make sure that the whole system is grounded and that the ground circuit is electrically continuous — without breaks.

If your circuitry is not of the three-wire grounding type, you can at least ground all of your appliances without going to the expense of installing completely new wiring. An inexpensive and easy way to ground appliances is to equip all three-prong appliance plugs with a grounded adapter plug. The plug goes into your two-blade receptacle, while its small grounding wire connects under the screw of the receptacle plate. **Cau-**

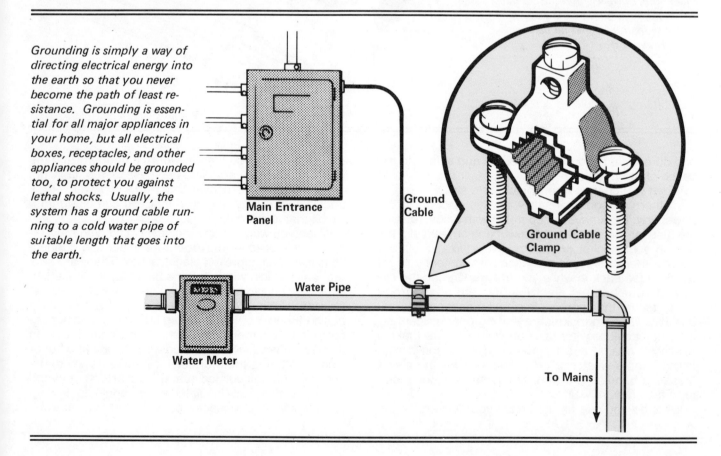

Grounding is simply a way of directing electrical energy into the earth so that you never become the path of least resistance. Grounding is essential for all major appliances in your home, but all electrical boxes, receptacles, and other appliances should be grounded too, to protect you against lethal shocks. Usually, the system has a ground cable running to a cold water pipe of suitable length that goes into the earth.

Main Entrance Panel

Ground Cable

Ground Cable Clamp

Water Pipe

Water Meter

To Mains

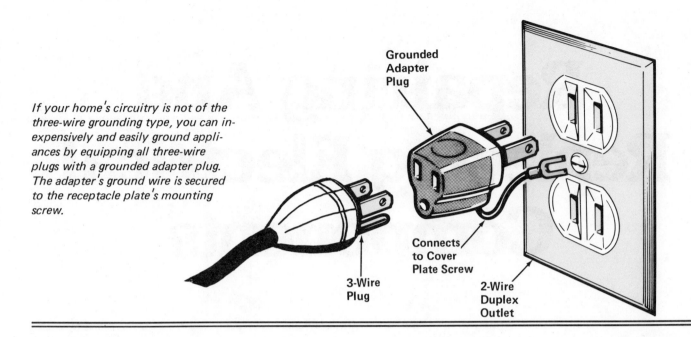

If your home's circuitry is not of the three-wire grounding type, you can inexpensively and easily ground appliances by equipping all three-wire plugs with a grounded adapter plug. The adapter's ground wire is secured to the receptacle plate's mounting screw.

Grounded Adapter Plug

Connects to Cover Plate Screw

3-Wire Plug

2-Wire Duplex Outlet

tion: For safety's sake, *never* remove the prong from a three-wire plug to make it fit a two-slot receptacle. Always use an adapter.

ELECTRICAL CODES

Residential electrical installations — and for that matter, other kinds as well — are frequently regulated by an electrical code. The best known, and the one in most widespread use today, is the National Electrical Code (NEC). In addition, there are any number of local electrical codes, based in large measure on the NEC and shortened, amplified or revised as necessary to suit local conditions and requirements. Most governmental authorities at all levels have adopted either the NEC in whole or in part, or some similar code to which all electrical installations under their jurisdiction must conform.

Where an electrical code is in force, and particularly where it is *enforced*, it is the responsibility of the home electrician to be familiar with its provisions as they apply to residential wiring and his own activities along those lines, and to follow them *explicitly*. This involves obtaining a copy of the applicable code and becoming familiar with it, drawing up whatever plans and specifications are required for the proposed work, obtaining a permit (and paying the attendant fee) to do the work, and finally having the completed job inspected by the proper authority. In most cases, simple repair work requires no permit or inspection, but circuit additions, rewiring, and such may. Note, too, that in some areas the homeowner cannot do any electrical work, even in his own home; all work must be done by a licensed electrician. This is the first point to check out.

In areas where no code is in force, following the provisions of the NEC is an excellent idea. Though this by no means ensures a superior installation that is fully efficient and fault-free, it is a good step in the right direction. The NEC is a distillation of many years of field experience, testing, research, and study, and by following its regulations and recommendations — required or not — you will greatly lessen your chances of going astray. Though definitely not an electrical wiring manual, nonetheless the NEC provides good guidelines for the proper application and installation of electrical equipment of all sorts and in practically all circumstances, and does so with one principal point in mind — safety. The code is the recognized authority for electrical installations everywhere, and following it makes good sense. Becoming familiar with the code will stand you in good stead, especially if you plan to go beyond the simple fix-it projects and become your own resident electrician.

Copies of local electrical codes can be obtained from your building department or electrical inspector's office, and perhaps may be available at your library. Copies of the NEC can be found in the same places in areas where that code is used, or it may be ordered direct from the National Fire Protection Association (NFPA).* The code is revised every four years; ask for the current edition. Other helpful publications, such as the *Handbook of the National Electrical Code,* which interprets the NEC, are also available from the NFPA.

---

*Publication Sales Department, 470 Atlantic Ave., Boston, MA 02210.

Repairing And Replacing Electrical Components

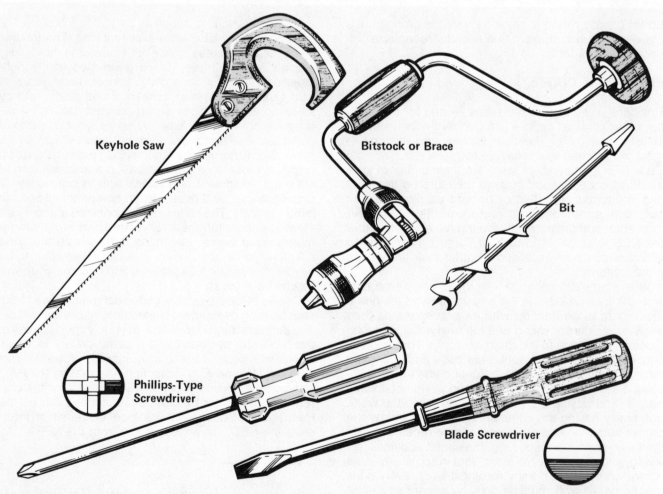

Keyhole Saw

Bitstock or Brace

Bit

Phillips-Type Screwdriver

Blade Screwdriver

To make simple electrical repairs, you will need a few simple hand tools. Most can be found in home workshops.

With skyrocketing prices for nearly everything in sight, it is a rare homeowner or apartment-dweller who does not feel the pinch of inflation. Nearly everyone, it seems, is trying to avoid unforeseen expenses like those occasioned by a breakdown in an electrical component. Yet these components — even ones of quality materials and workmanship — cannot last forever. Lamps stop lighting, doorbells stop ringing, and receptacles stop holding plugs; these failures occur in the normal course of events.

What options are available to someone faced with a malfunctioning electrical component? An electrician, of course, can be called in, but then the cost of repair or replacement gets really steep. The logical solution for many simple repairs is, therefore, to do it yourself. Generally speaking, these electrical tasks require only those tools that you are likely to have around the house, and they demand no more technical expertise than reading and following directions. Just be sure that you make safety your first priority, and you will be amazed at what you can do to maintain, renovate, and upgrade the electrical devices in your home.

TOOLS

To make simple electrical repairs, you will need a few simple hand tools. The more extensive and complex your repair work, and the deeper you go into projects such as adding circuits or perhaps even rewiring your house, the more tools you will need. Most, however, are inexpensive and can be found in most home workshops; there are a few specialized tools that you might want or eventually need, but those are also usually inexpensive.

The first requisite is a selection of screwdrivers. These should be good quality tools with insulated handles. You will need at least three sizes for slotted screws, as well as at least one Phillips-type screwdriver. You will also want a hammer — an ordinary carpenter's claw hammer will do — a pair of slip-joint

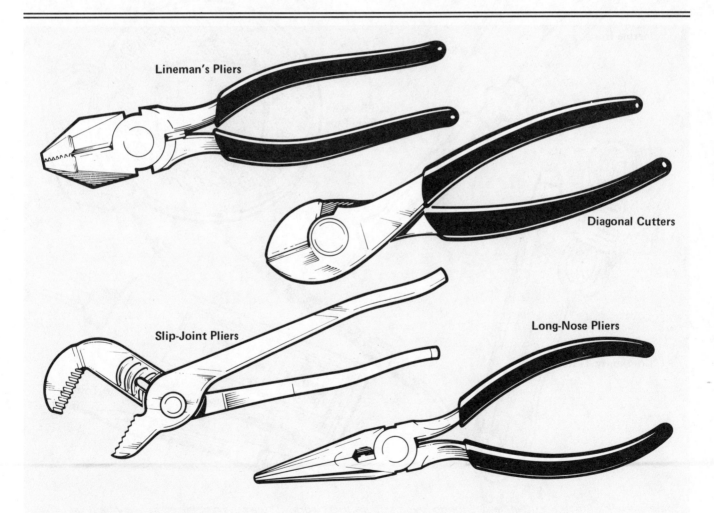

Lineman's Pliers

Diagonal Cutters

Slip-Joint Pliers

Long-Nose Pliers

There are many types of cutters and pliers. Some that are commonly used in electrical work are illustrated.

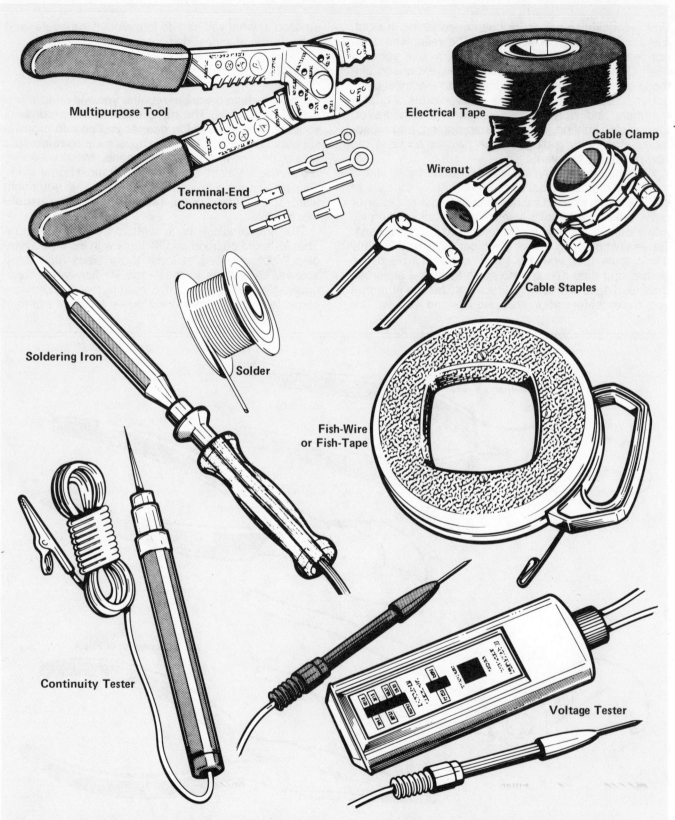

Multipurpose Tool

Electrical Tape

Cable Clamp

Terminal-End Connectors

Wirenut

Cable Staples

Soldering Iron

Solder

Fish-Wire or Fish-Tape

Continuity Tester

Voltage Tester

Some specialized tools are often needed for do-it-yourself electrical work. These can be obtained at many hardware stores and electrical supply houses.

pliers, and a pair of adjustable water-pump pliers. One or two adjustable wrenches will come in handy. Your electrical toolbox should also contain a tape measure, putty knife, keyhole saw, perhaps a wood chisel, a small torpedo level, either a bitstock or a ⅜-inch electric drill, and a selection of drill bits.

But you will need some specialized tools, too, which you can obtain at any electrical supply house and some hardware stores. Equip yourself with a pair of electrician's diagonal cutters with insulated handles — the kind that has stubby, wide jaws works better than one with long, narrow jaws. An ordinary utility knife is fine for slitting the outer plastic jacket of Type NM or Type UF cable, but for stripping the insulation off the conductors, you should use a wire stripper made for this purpose. Another special tool you will need is a circuit tester to determine whether a circuit is live or dead. Or, you can purchase a more sophisticated — and more expensive — tester that will actually measure voltages and currents.

If you will be working with metal-clad types of cable, a special armored-cable cutter will save you a lot of time. Installing EMT (electrical metallic tubing) or rigid conduit requires a hacksaw or a pipe cutter, a pipe or tubing bender, and a file and a reamer for deburring cut ends. Conduit work also calls for pipe-threading equipment. If you will be working with modern circuits having three-slot outlets and an equipment grounding loop, a polarity-checking device is very useful. You may need an electrician's snake or fish-wire for fishing cables through walls and ceilings, and a continuity tester for determining whether a dead circuit is open or closed, and for checking ground loops.

RESTORING A CIRCUIT

The overload devices — fuses or circuit breakers — in your electrical system are there for a purpose, to blow or trip if the circuit should become overloaded. When that happens, as it does from time to time in just about every home, what do you do?

The first step should be taken *before* a circuit trips off. If you have not already done so, make a list of all the branch circuits by number and the locations to which the circuits go in your home. Then you can discover which outlets and fixtures are on a particular branch circuit. If you are unsure as to whether the list is accurate and complete, you can verify it through a very simple procedure. Just remove a fuse or trip a circuit breaker to its "off" position, and check to see what equipment or devices are deenergized. Of course, it is easy to see when a ceiling light goes out; but you can determine the status of an outlet just as easily by plugging in a lamp — a small night-light that you insert directly in the outlet is an ideal indicator. Once you know exactly which outlets, fixtures and appliances are connected to a particular branch circuit, write all the

information on a card and attach the card to the inside of the main entrance panel's door.

When a circuit goes off, there may be some visual or audible indication of the trouble spot, such as a bright flare from a lamp or a sputtering, sparking sound from an appliance, that will immediately lead you to the source of the trouble. If so, disconnect the faulty equipment. If not, arm yourself with a flashlight, if necessary, and go to the main entrance panel. Check to see which fuse is blown or which breaker has tripped, note the circuit number, and determine from your information card which outlets, appliances, and lighting fixtures are on the circuit. Then disconnect everything on that circuit that you can, and inspect those that you cannot easily disconnect for signs (or odors) of malfunction. Then replace the fuse or reset the breaker. If the circuit "holds in," perhaps something that you disconnected is faulty; check for short circuits or other problems. (If there is no evidence of electrical fault, the problem may be an overload — too much current draw for the circuit to handle. Remove some of the loads from that circuit.)

If the new fuse blows or the circuit breaker refuses to reset, the problem lies in equipment that is still connected or in the circuit cable itself. The greater likelihood of malfunction lies with the still-connected items, so tackle those first, examining each for faults until you find the offending equipment. If the circuit still goes out when there are no loads connected to it, the wiring itself is faulty, probably because of a short in a junction or outlet box, or possibly in the cable itself. With the circuit dead, start at the far end of the line and inspect all of the connections.

If there is no visible evidence of a problem, you will have to check each segment of the circuit, section by section, with a continuity tester. Make certain that the circuit is still deenergized, because a continuity tester can never be used on an energized circuit. Be sure that nothing is connected to the circuit segments during this procedure. Otherwise, you may obtain a false reading. Start at the panel end of the circuit and touch the probe leads of the tester to the bare ends of the wires. If the tester lights up, or you get a reading on the meter dial, the circuit has continuity and there are no breaks or loose connections in the line; that part of the circuit is alright. If the tester does not register, there is a break somewhere. You will have to disconnect each segment of the circuit, section by section, and check each until you obtain a clear reading (no light or meter reading). This procedure will isolate the fault, which you can then repair to permanently clear the circuit.

A circuit breaker is a remarkably trouble-free device, but once in a while a breaker does fail. The result is that the circuit will not energize, even though it is fault-free. If a circuit goes out and the circuit breaker itself has a distinctive, burnt-plastic odor, the trip handle is loose and wobbly, the reset mechanism seems all afloat in-

EMERGENCY BLACKOUT KIT

1. *Candles or oil lamps and matches for area lighting.*
2. *Flashlight, battery lantern or other auxiliary light source for trouble-shooting.*
3. *Correct and up-to-date circuit directory posted on main entrance panel door.*
4. *Tool kit with appropriate tools for making electrical repairs.*
5. *Circuit tester, preferably the voltage-readout type of tester.*
6. *Spare parts:*

For Fuse Boxes
- *Two each replacement plug fuses of each amperage rating in use, preferably Type S.*
- *Four each replacement cartridge fuses, including main fuses, of each amperage rating in use.*

For Circuit Breaker Boxes
- *One replacement single-pole circuit breaker of a rating equal to the smallest size in use or one of each size in use.*
- *One replacement double-pole circuit breaker of each amperage rating in use.*

General Parts
- *Selection of light bulbs.*
- *One replacement duplex receptable to match existing units.*
- *One replacement single-pole switch to match existing units.*
- *One replacement three-way or other special switches to match existing units.*
- *Miscellaneous supplies — wirenuts, electrician's tape, etc.*

---

ternally or if the breaker rattles when you shake it, it has probably failed. You can make certain by checking it with a continuity tester. The only remedy, of course, is to replace the circuit breaker; they are not repairable.

COPING WITH A POWER OUTAGE

What do you do when all power in the house goes off? Usually, this is due to a general power outage in the entire neighborhood or district, but sometimes the problem lies in the individual residential wiring system.

The first step is to see whether the outage is a general one or yours alone. If it occurs at night, look around the neighborhood to see if everyone else's lights are off. In the daytime, call a neighbor to see if others are affected. Or, if you have a circuit breaker-type of main disconnect, check to see whether it has tripped to the "off" position. If the main entrance is fused, pull the fuse block out and slip the fuses free. Check them with a continuity tester to see if they are blown or still good (with a probe lead touched to each end of the fuse, the tester light will come on if the fuse is good).

If you determine that the trouble is a general power outage, all you can do is call the power company (by this time, others probably already will have done so). If your main breaker is still in the "on" position or both main fuses are good, but your neighbors have power and you do not, the fault lies between your main entrance panel and the power transmission lines. The reason could be a downed service drop, a faulty or overloaded pole transformer or some such problem; call the power company, because this part of your system is their responsibility.

If you find a tripped main breaker or blown main fuses in your main entrance panel, the problem lies within the house and may be a serious one. *Do not*

attempt to reset the breaker; replacing the fuses will probably be futile. The difficulty may be a general overload — you are simply using more total current than the main breaker can pass. Or, there may be a dead short somewhere in the house.

The first step is to go back through the house and turn off everything that you can. Then, in the case of a circuit breaker panel, flip all of the breakers to the "off" position, and reset the main breaker to the "on" position. One by one, trip the branch circuit breakers back on. One of them may either fail to reset or the main breaker will again trip off as you trip a branch breaker on — the source of the trouble lies in that circuit, and the circuit will have to be cleared of the fault.

If all of the breakers go back on and the main breaker holds in, you are faced with two possibilities. One is that something you disconnected earlier is faulty. Go back along the line, inspect each item for possible fault, and plug each one back in. Sooner or later you will discover which one is causing the problem, either visually or by the fact that a breaker trips out when you reconnect the item. The other and more likely possibility is a general, system-wide overloading. This is characterized by recurrent tripping-out of the main breaker when practically everything in the house is running but there are actually no electrical faults to be found. There are two remedies to this problem. One is to lessen the total electrical load; this should be done in any case as at least a short-term measure. The other is to install a new, larger main entrance panel, along with new branch circuits to serve areas in the house of heavy electrical usage and to help share the total load.

The trouble-shooting approach is much the same if the main panel is the fused type, except that you will need to have a supply of fuses on hand. First pull all of the cartridge fuses and unscrew all of the plug fuses in the panel. Replace the main fuses and put the fuse block back into place. Then, one by one, replace each fuse or set of fuses until the one that is causing the outage blows out again. That is the circuit that must be cleared. General overloading, however, will cause the main fuses to go out again.

Specific testing for general overload is a simple matter, and is most easily done with a snap-around volt-ohm-ammeter, an instrument that snaps around the cable and provides you with a direct amperage reading while the line is under load — no interconnections are needed. Use the test instrument according to the manufacturer's instructions, and take readings at each of the two main incoming lines in the main entrance panel at various times of the day, or after turning on just about all of the power-consuming devices in the house that might normally be operating concurrently. Note the highest reading obtained from either line, and compare it to the capacity rating of the main disconnect. If, for instance, your main panel is rated at 100 amperes and is equipped with a 100-ampere main breaker, and your readings show a maximum draw of 97 amperes, that leg is running right on the verge of trouble. Just a bit more load and the main disconnect is sure to go out. On the other hand, if the greatest draw you can manage is 90 amperes, you are safe enough. But, you will not be able to add another circuit or a major appliance without running into difficulties, unless the other main leg is only lightly loaded and you can shuffle circuits around to effect a better balance between the two.

CHECKING OUTLET POLARITY

Residential wiring systems installed a few years ago or earlier use a two-wire system in the 110-120-volt branch circuits. One conductor is "hot" and the other is a neutral, and the latter may serve as a ground too. But unfortunately, it usually does not, thereby creating a potentially hazardous situation. You can easily tell if your circuits are of this type by noting the plug socket configuration in your convenience outlets — there will be only two slots. Modern wiring calls for the installation of a third conductor, a bare wire called the equipment grounding conductor. Receptacles used with this system have three openings: two vertical rectangular slots and a third, rounded aperture centered above them. Either two-prong or three-prong plugs can be plugged into these receptacles, but only the three-pronged kind will carry the equipment grounding line to the electrical equipment. Also, one of the vertical slots is different in size than the other, so that the newer types of two-pronged plugs can only be inserted in one direction. This insures you that the equipment being connected will be properly polarized, hot side to hot side and neutral to neutral.

Caution: In the interest of proper operation and safety, it is essential that all receptacles on each circuit

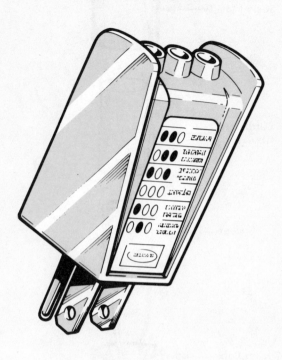

Receptacle Analyzer

To make certain that receptacles are installed properly—with the individual conductors going to the correct terminals—you can use an instrument, such as this plug-in analyzer, to check the outlet's polarity.

be installed with the individual conductors going to the correct terminals, so that there are no polarity reversals along the line that would negate the effectiveness of the system. Unfortunately, they are not always connected in this manner, even in new wiring systems installed by professional electricians. You can easily and quickly check out your receptacles with a small, inexpensive tester called a polarity checker that is designed for this purpose. It looks like a fancy three-pronged plug, and contains three neon-bulb indicators. Simply plug the checker into a receptacle; the lights will tell you if the polarity is correct, and if not, which lines are reversed. If there is a reversal, turn the circuit off, pull the receptacle out of the box, and switch the wires to the proper terminals. Or, if the equipment-grounding circuit is open (discontinuous), you can trace the circuit until you find the disconnection or missing link and reconnect it to restore the effectiveness of the circuit.

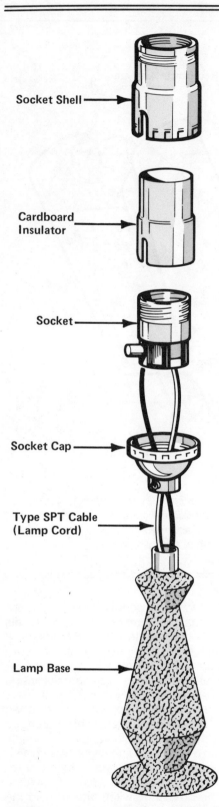

Socket Shell

Cardboard
Insulator

Socket

Socket Cap

Type SPT Cable
(Lamp Cord)

Lamp Base

Fixing a lamp is not difficult. Electrical components are inexpensive and easy to replace. The parts that are most often responsible for the lamp failing to work properly are the socket, cord and plug.

REWIRING A LAMP

There is no reason why you must live with lamps that do not function properly, and may be dangerous, too.

The plug, cord, and socket — the parts that are probably causing the lamp to malfunction — are easy and inexpensive to replace. You can get them at any well-stocked hardware store, and certainly at any store that specializes in electrical parts. Why, for example, should you put up with the annoyance of a plug that is misshapen or broken, or that fails to make a satisfactory electrical connection in the outlet? With a quick-clamp plug — the kind that eliminates the need for fastening wires under terminal screws — you can have a new one on in seconds.

You can install a new socket just about as easily. Replacement sockets come in various finishes — brass or nickel metal, and black or brown plastic — and you should be able to find a socket that approximates the color tone of the remainder of the lamp's fixture. And if you plan to replace a socket, why not consider putting in a three-way socket for greater lighting versatility? Wiring a three-way socket is as simple as wiring the standard on/off version.

Lamp cord is known as Type SPT, but if you ask for "zip cord" at a hardware or electrical supply store, you can get what you need. The #18 size is satisfactory for most lamp applications. It is available in many colors, the most common being black, brown, white, and transparent. Match the cord color to the lamp, and order a sufficient length for your needs. The customary length is 6 feet, but you can install as much cord as the distance between the lamp and the receptacle (add the length of the cord hidden in the lamp, plus 1 foot for attachments to socket and plug, and for some slack) dictates. It is better — in terms of safety and appearance — to have an adequate length of cord than to compensate for a short one with an extension cord.

Here Is What You Will Need

Materials

- Length of Type SPT lamp cord
- Replacement lamp socket (optional)
- Quick-clamp or screw-terminal plug
- Rosin-core solder (optional)

Tools

- Screwdrivers
- Electrician's diagonal cutters
- Wire stripper
- Electrical tape
- Soldering iron (optional)
- Utility pliers (optional)

Better yet, keep all cords as short as possible.

To rewire a lamp, first pull the plug from the electrical outlet; never do any work while the lamp is connected. Remove the shade, unscrew the bulb, and squeeze the socket shell at the switch to separate the shell and cardboard insulator from the socket cap. *Do not* use a screwdriver to pry the socket apart if you plan to reuse the socket. Pull the socket out of the shell as far as the attached wire permits, but if that amount is not enough to work with, push some of the cord up from the bottom of the lamp for additional slack.

Loosen the socket's terminal screws, and remove the cord wires from under them. If the lamp is a small one and the cord goes through in a fairly straight path, you should be able to slide the old wire out and easily feed the new wire through from one end or the other. But if the lamp is large and the cord takes a few twists and turns along its internal path, your job can be more difficult. If the old cord offers any resistance at all to coming free, do not tug on it. Check to see if you can disassemble the lamp to make removal easier. Also check to see if the cord is tied in a knot to prevent it from being pulled out at its base. To remove a tight cord, cut the wire off about 12 inches from the lamp's base, slit the cord's two conductors apart, and strip about an inch of insulation off the ends; do the same to one end of the new length of cord. Twist the bare new and old conductor ends together and fold the twists flat along the cord, then wrap plastic electrician's tape around the splice in as small a lump as you can, with the wrapping smooth and tapered so that it will not catch or hang up on anything. Pull on the old cord from the top of the fixture and work the new cord through; push on the new cord from the bottom at the same time to aid the process. When you have a sufficient length of new cord through at the top, clip the wire off.

Once you pass the new cord through the lamp, split the end so that you have about 3 inches of separated conductors. Strip about an inch of insulation from the end of each conductor and twist the strands of each together. If you wish, you can tin the strands with a soldering iron — use only rosin-core solder to fuse the tiny strands into a solid conductor end. What you must avoid doing, though, is nicking the strands when you strip the insulation — a distinct possibility if you use a knife or electrician's diagonal cutters for the job. Instead, use a wire stripper with the correct size of cutting slots for the conductors for this and any other insulation removal task; this tool is designed to remove insulation without damaging the wire.

Loop each of the bare wire ends under their respective socket screws with the loops curled in a clockwise direction. Then tighten the screws. The clockwise loop will pull the wire tighter under the screw head; a counterclockwise loop tends to force the wire out from under the screw head. When both screw heads are snugged firmly over the bare conductor ends, clip off any excess

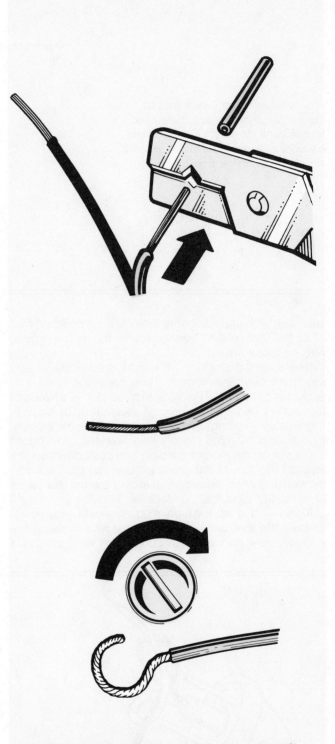

To connect a wire under a terminal screw, strip 3/4 inch of insulation off the end (top), twist the strands together (center), and loop the end (bottom) in a clockwise direction so that the terminal screw will pull the wire tighter under the screw head when it is tightened.

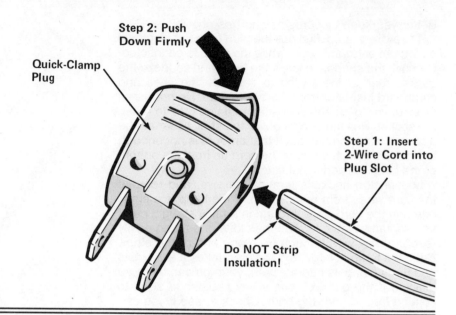

A quick-clamp plug is very easy to install. Metal prongs inside the plug bite through the cord's insulation and pierce the copper wires inside to make the electrical connection.

Quick-Clamp Plug

Step 2: Push Down Firmly

Step 1: Insert 2-Wire Cord into Plug Slot

Do NOT Strip Insulation!

bare wire with your diagonal cutters. It is important that all of the uninsulated wire be under the screw heads, with no loose strands.

Now slide the shell over the cardboard insulator and slip them over the socket. Then snap the shell and socket into the cap. That is all there is to it — at least at the socket end of the lamp. A new cord, of course, requires a new plug. A quick-clamp plug is the easiest kind to connect; you merely stick the end of the cord into a slot on the side of the plug and push down on the lever at the top. Metal prongs inside the plug will bite through the cord insulation, piercing the copper wires to make the electrical connection.

If you use a screw-type plug, however, you must prepare the wire ends just as you did when making the socket screw connections. Loop each wire around a

prong before tightening the bare end under the screw head. The loops keep the wires apart and also make it more difficult to loosen the connections by pulling on the cord. Of course, you should never disconnect a lamp — or any other portable electrical device — by yanking the cord out of the wall socket, but the loops will give some strain support in such circumstances. Tighten the wires under the screw heads, and clip off any excess uninsulated conductor before you put the plug in a receptacle.

REPLACING APPLIANCE CORDS

Replacing the cords on appliances, power tools and other equipment is generally a simple chore. Some special cords can, and should be, bought as complete

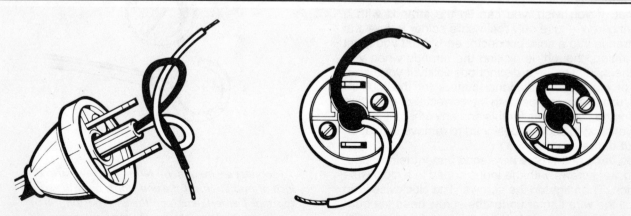

On screw-type plugs, insert the cord, tie the wires into a knot, and pull the knot down into the plug. Then, loop each wire around a prong before tightening the bare end under the screw head. This helps keep the wires from touching each other accidentally.

Lamp Trouble-Shooting Chart

PROBLEMS	CAUSES	REPAIRS
Lamp does not light	1. Lamp unplugged.	1. Plug lamp in.
	2. Circuit dead.	2. Restore circuit.
	3. Bulb loose.	3. Tighten bulb.
	4. Bulb burned out.	4. Replace bulb.
	5. Loose connection at plug or socket.	5. Trace and repair.
	6. Defective wall switch.	6. Replace switch.
	7. Defective socket switch.	7. Replace socket.
	8. Defective center contact in socket.	8. Pry contact up or replace socket.
	9. Broken conductor in line cord.	9. Repair or replace line cord.
Lamp blows fuse or trips circuit breaker	1. Overloaded circuit.	1. Check total load on circuit. If overloaded, transfer some equipment to a different circuit.
	2. Short circuit in socket, in cord or in lamp wiring.	2. Replace socket and cord. Rewire carefully to make sure no bare wires touch each other or any metal parts of the lamp.
Lamp flickers when moved or touched	1. Lamp bulb loose in socket.	1. Tighten bulb.
	2. Loose connection, usually where line cord wires are fastened under the terminal screws on the lamp socket.	2. First, make sure lamp is unplugged; then, take socket apart and inspect wire connections under the screws. Tighten or, if so indicated, cut off a short length of cord and reattach wire ends.
	3. Defective contacts or faulty switch in socket.	3. First, make sure lamp is unplugged; then, remove the socket and replace it with a new one.
	4. Defective lamp cord.	4. Replace cord. Rewire carefully to make sure no bare wires touch each other or any metal parts of the lamp.

sets, with a plug attached to one end and special connection terminals attached to the other end. General-purpose cords can be fashioned from a separate plug, a length of an appropriate type of cord, and perhaps connection terminals as well. Electric range and clothes iron cords exemplify the former type, table saw and food mixer cords the latter.

Often, the hardest part of the job is in trying to determine how the equipment comes apart so that you can remove the old cord and attach a new one. Sometimes, all you have to do is remove the cover from a connection box, as on a water pump. In other instances, like an electric drill, the unit itself must be partially disassembled before you can reach the terminals. In nearly all cases, the cord will be held in place by a clamp or by a fitted strain-relief device. To remove the cord, undo the terminal screws or pull the pressure connectors apart, loosen the clamp or remove the strain-relief device, and withdraw the cord. Installation of the new cord is merely a reverse procedure. Be sure to save the

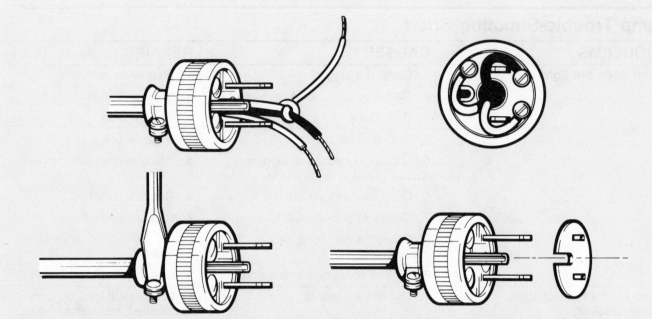

Power tools and some appliances have three-wire grounded plugs. To install a new plug, tie the "hot" and neutral wires into a knot (top, left). Loop the "hot" and neutral wires around their respective prongs, and the ground wire around its prong (top, right), before securing all three to their terminal screws. Then, tighten—if present—the plug's screw-clamp (bottom, left). Finally, slide the cardboard insulating disc over the prongs (bottom, right).

strain-relief device and replace it on the new cord. If you have to destroy the strain-relief device to remove it, fit a new one of the same or a similar type.

In some equipment, the conductor ends are tinned and looped around the terminal screws just as in a lamp, and making new connections is easy. In other devices, solderless connection terminals may be clamped to the old cord, and you will have to fit replacement terminals to the new cord. This requires terminals of a matching kind plus a special tool called a "staker" or "crimper." You can find these tools at automotive or electrical supply stores. In a few cases, the terminals may be soldered to the conductor ends. You can replace them with either soldered or solderless connection terminals. However, never use soldered terminals on any heat-producing or high-current-draw equipment — there is a good chance that the solder can melt.

WALL AND CEILING FIXTURES

As far as the electrical work is concerned, replacing a lighting fixture is relatively simple. You can even put in fluorescent lighting where you now have incandescent fixtures without encountering any great problems. In fact, the worst difficulties you will probably face involve not the electrical connections but rather the mechanical complexities of attaching a new fixture to older mounting hardware.

Caution: If you are going to replace or repair any lighting fixture, the first thing to do is deenergize the appropriate electrical circuit. In a house that is properly wired (with switching done in the "hot" wire), turning off the wall switch deenergizes the fixture. Nevertheless, if you have any doubts whatsoever regarding the wiring in your house, deenergize the entire circuit by pulling the appropriate fuse or tripping the proper circuit breaker.

Replacing an Incandescent Fixture

With the fixture (or the entire circuit) deenergized and your alternate light source in position, take off the globe, unscrew the bulb(s), and disassemble all mounting hardware. Usually there are just screws holding the fixture against the wall or ceiling, but you may discover that a particular lighting fixture possesses no visible mounting hardware at all. If you do not see any screws or bolts, look for a decorative feature that probably doubles as a fastener. Take off the mounting hardware and withdraw the fixture from the electrical box.

Disconnect the lamp fixture wires from the circuit wires. You may find that the wire joint is fused together with old insulating tape that defies easy removal. In such a case, you will find it simpler to cut the wires close to the tape. **Caution:** If the wire insulation, or the conductors, coming into the electrical box is brittle or frayed, that part of the circuit or switch loop should be rewired. Once you remove the old fixture, you can examine the electrical box — as well as the new fixture — to determine which of the following installation procedures you should use:

Standard Electrical Box. Make sure that you have about ¾ inch of bare copper conductor on the end of each line wire before you start to connect the wires of your new lighting fixture. If necessary, remove enough insulation from the line wires so that you can twist each line wire end together with the end of each light fixture wire, white to white and black to black. Screw a wirenut tightly over each pair of twisted ends. Hold onto the fixture to support the weight until you attach the mounting screws; otherwise, you might break a connection or damage the fixture wires.

If the fixture has more than one socket, connect one black wire from each of the sockets to the black line wire, and the white wire from each socket to the white line wire. In other words, connect all the sockets in parallel to both line wires. Naturally, three or four socket wires joined to a line wire would require that you use a larger solderless connector.

That is really all there is to do insofar as the electrical connections are concerned. Now all you have to do is mount the fixture. Usually, mounting screws of the proper length will be included with your new lamp fixture, but screws that are 2 or 2½ inches long should take care of most fixtures. Insert the screws into the attachment screw holes in the electrical box, and turn each of them four or five times — just enough so that they hold in place. Examine the pan, or base, of the new fixture; you will see two or more sets of keyhole-shaped slots. Mount the fixture by passing the fixture's keyhole slots over the screw heads. Then, rotate the fixture enough so that the screws go into the narrow parts of the keyhole slots.

Tighten the screws, but do not overtighten them;

Here Is What You Will Need

Materials

- Replacement lamp fixture
- Solderless connectors
- Fixture hanging hardware (as required)
- Miscellaneous hardware (as required)

Tools

- Screwdrivers
- Electrician's diagonal cutters
- Auxiliary light source
- Wire stripper
- Pliers
- Stepladder (optional)

they should just be snug enough to hold the fixture firmly in place. If you tighten the mounting screws too much, you may distort and misalign the fixture. With the fixture mounted properly, screw in the bulbs, attach the globe, and replace the fuse or trip the circuit breaker back on. Flip the wall switch. If the fixture lights up, the job is finished. If nothing happens, go back and figure out which connection needs remaking.

Electrical Box with No Threaded Ears. The electrical connections in a box with no threaded ears are exactly the same as those in the standard electrical box. The only difference is in mounting the new fixture. After you remove the old fixture, fasten a fixture strap to the threaded stud inside the electrical box with a locknut that fits the stud threads. Frequently, a manufacturer packages a strap with a fixture, but if you have to buy one, make sure that the screw holes are spaced so that they match the new fixture's mounting holes. Insert the screws in the threaded holes at the outer ends of the fixture strap, and turn them two or three times.

Connect the circuit line wires to the fixture wires, mount the fixture in place, and tighten the mounting screws. Before you tighten the screws completely, however, make sure that all the wires and solderless connectors are tucked up inside the fixture and the electrical box. They should never be squeezed between the fixture strap and the fixture. Screw in the bulb(s), attach the globe, and replace the fuse or trip the circuit breaker back on.

Pipe-Supported Fixtures. A replacement fixture that includes a globe held by a pipe running through its center demands other installation procedures. After you remove the old fixture, fasten a fixture strap firmly to the electrical box. Generally speaking, the manufacturer packages a fixture strap with a new lamp, but if you must buy one, ask for a strap that has a center hole threaded to accommodate a ⅛-inch pipe. Connect the line wires to the fixture wires, and turn a locknut onto one threaded end of the mounting pipe. Now, while holding the fixture body up in its final mounting position, run the pipe through the hole in the fixture and thread it into the fixture strap far enough so that it holds the fixture firmly in place.

Screw a bulb in the fixture socket and restore the circuit to make sure that you installed everything properly. If you did, attach the globe with the threaded cap that comes with the fixture. You may find that the globe does not fit properly, but you can remedy this situation easily. Just tighten or loosen the pipe a few turns from the fixture hanger, but be sure to adjust the position of the locknut to keep the fixture secure against the ceiling. Keep working with the pipe and locknut until precisely the right length of pipe hangs down to just accommodate the globe and its mounting knob.

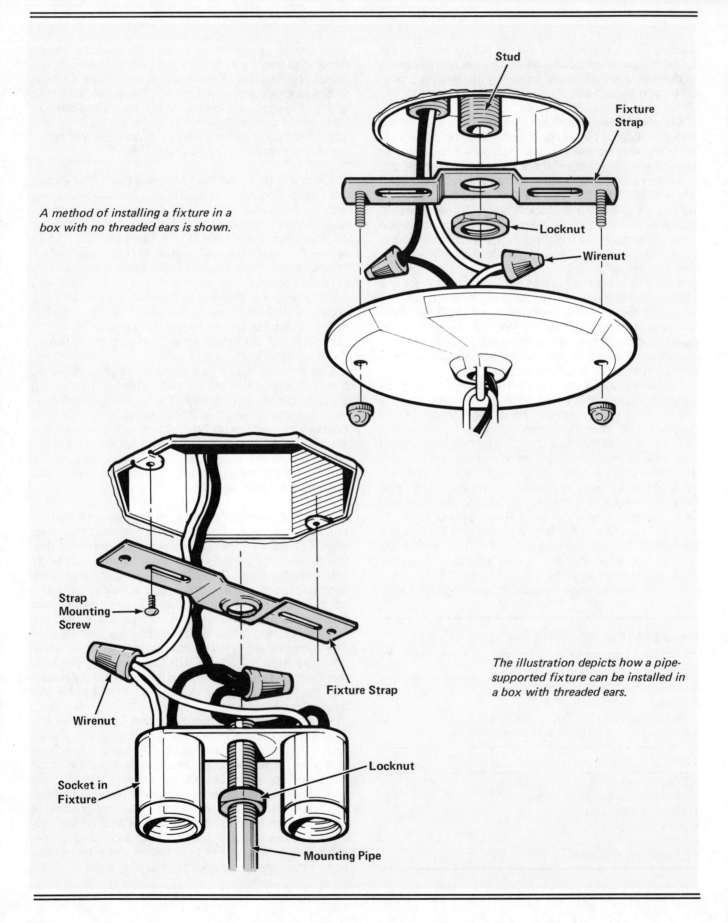

Stud

Fixture Strap

A method of installing a fixture in a box with no threaded ears is shown.

Locknut

Wirenut

Strap Mounting Screw

Fixture Strap

The illustration depicts how a pipe-supported fixture can be installed in a box with threaded ears.

Wirenut

Socket in Fixture

Locknut

Mounting Pipe

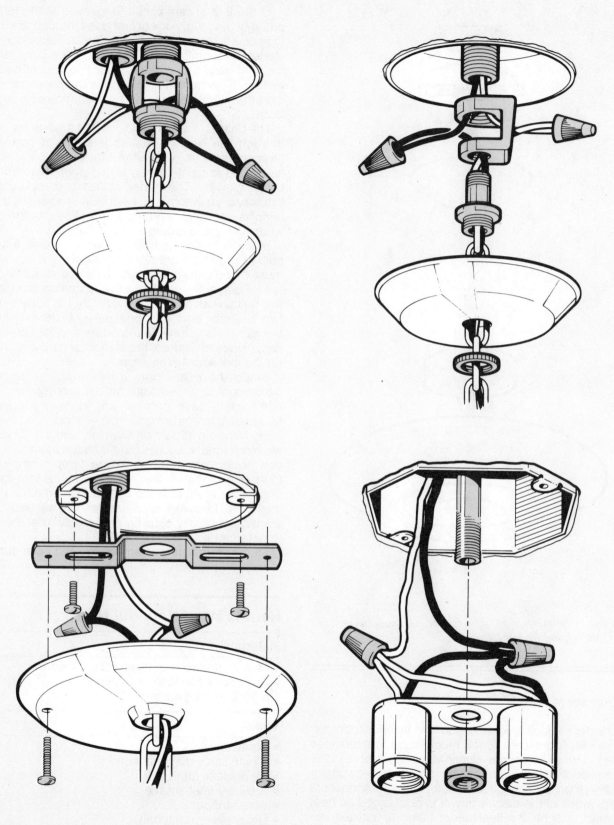

There are many ways in which lighting fixtures can be installed. Some variations are illustrated.

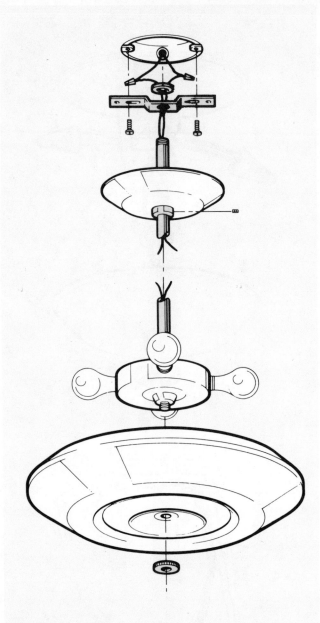

In the fluorescent circuit, beginning at the left-hand prong of the plug, current first goes through the ballast, then one of the lamp filaments, the closed switch in the starter, through the other filament in the lamp, and out the right-hand prong of the plug. The current heats the two small elements in the ends of the fluorescent tube; then the starter opens, and current flows through the lamp.

The ballast is a magnetic coil that adjusts the current through the bulb. It makes a surge of current arc through the bulb when the starter opens, and then keeps the current flowing at the right value once the bulb is glowing. The starter, at least in most fluorescent fixtures, is an automatic switch. Once it senses that the lamp is glowing, it stays open. The starter closes whenever you deenergize the fixture.

Many fluorescent fixtures contain more than one bulb to provide a greater amount of light. Such lamps must have individual starters and ballasts for each bulb. Frequently, you find a fixture that appears to have two bulbs working off one ballast, but actually there are two ballasts built into one case. Fixtures with four bulbs, similarly, have four starters and four ballasts. In some kinds of fixtures, the starters are built in and cannot be individually replaced.

Since there are only three principal parts in a fluorescent lamp — bulb, ballast, and starter — you can usually take care of any repairs yourself. All fluorescent lamps grow dimmer with age, and they may even begin to flicker or flash on and off. These are warning signals, and you should heed them as soon as you notice any change in the lamp's normal performance. A dim bulb usually requires replacement, and failure to replace the bulb can strain other parts of the fixture. Likewise, repeated flashing will wear out the starter, eventually causing the insulation at the starter to deteriorate.

Fluorescent fixtures can be serviced quite simply by

In this installation, a multiple-socket, pipe-supported fixture is hung from a fixture strap.

Fluorescent Lamps

Consider replacing some of your old incandescent fixtures with fluorescent lamps. Fluorescent light provides even and shadow-free illumination. Best of all, the fluorescent bulb renders much more light — watt for watt — than an incandescent bulb. In the incandescent bulb, much of the electric power is discharged as heat instead of light; the fluorescent bulb, in contrast, remains fairly cool.

Here Is What You Will Need

Materials

- New or replacement fluorescent fixture
- Solderless connectors (wirenuts)
- Mounting hardware

Tools

- Screwdrivers
- Electrician's diagonal cutters
- Stepladder (optional)
- Auxiliary light source
- Wire stripper
- Utility pliers (optional)

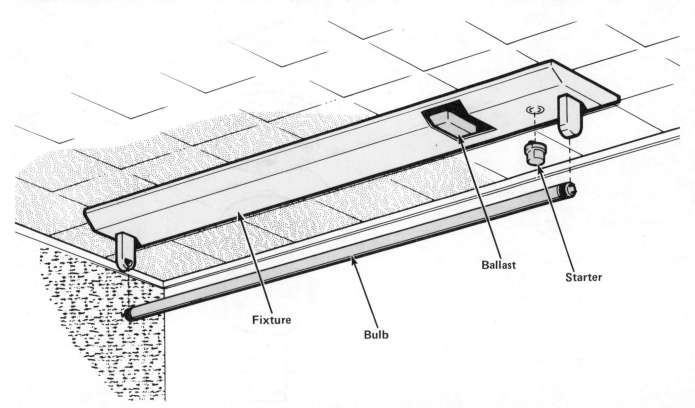

A fluorescent fixture has three main parts—bulb, ballast, and starter. Usually, a do-it-yourselfer can take care of any repairs.

the substitution method. If you suspect that a part may be defective, install a new part. Start with the fluorescent tube or bulb. You can either install a new one or, if you are in doubt, test the old bulb in another fluorescent fixture. Doing both gives you double verification. If the problem is not in the bulb, change the starter, if possible. Fluorescent lamp starters are rated according to wattage, and it is important that you match the right starter to the bulb in your fixture.

The ballast is also rated according to wattage, and a replacement ballast — like a replacement starter — must match the wattage of the bulb, and the type of fixture. The ballast is the least likely part to fail, however, and it is the most difficult to replace. Therefore, when you start the substitution repair method, leave the ballast for last; but if neither the bulb nor the starter proves to be defective, the problem must be the ballast. To replace a faulty ballast, you must deenergize the circuit, disassemble the fixture, transfer wires from the old ballast to the new one (one at a time to avoid an incorrect connection), and finally reassemble the fixture.

If you are considering going to all the trouble involved in installing a new ballast, you should give some thought to putting in an entirely new fixture. Your old fluorescent fixture suffers the same aging effects —

both in appearance and performance — as does your outmoded incandescent fixture. Of course, you can also replace an old incandescent lamp with a new fluorescent model. Either replacement is possible and well within the capabilities of the do-it-yourselfer.

Caution: Before you begin, be sure to deenergize the old fixture. If your home is wired properly (with switching done only in the "hot" wire), merely turning off the wall switch will deenergize the fixture. If you are uncertain about the wiring, however, be sure to remove the circuit's fuse or trip the circuit breaker.

Remove the old hardware that holds the existing lamp fixture (either incandescent or fluorescent) in place, and disconnect the lamp wires from the circuit line wires. Then, disassemble the new fluorescent lamp as far as necessary to gain access to the fixture wires, and connect them to the line wires with wirenuts, or crimp-type solderless connectors. Maintain the wire color continuity: white to white, black to black.

Position the fixture against the ceiling, and fasten it with the screws that are packaged with the new lamp. You may have to reassemble the fixture either before or after mounting it. This depends on the fixture's style. Once you get the lamp back together, restore the power, and turn on your new fluorescent lighting fixture.

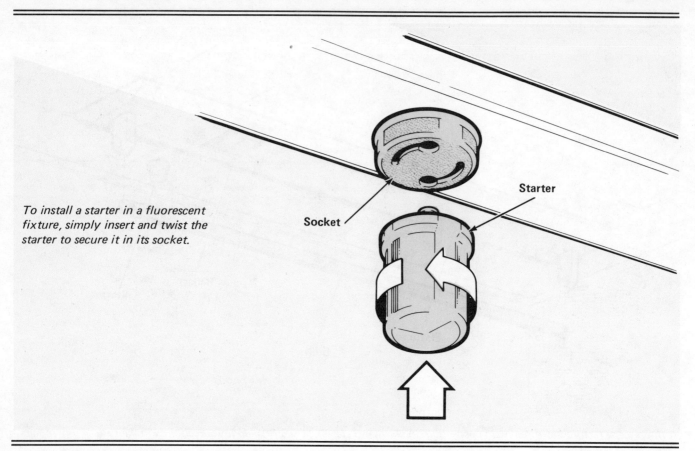

To install a starter in a fluorescent fixture, simply insert and twist the starter to secure it in its socket.

Socket

Starter

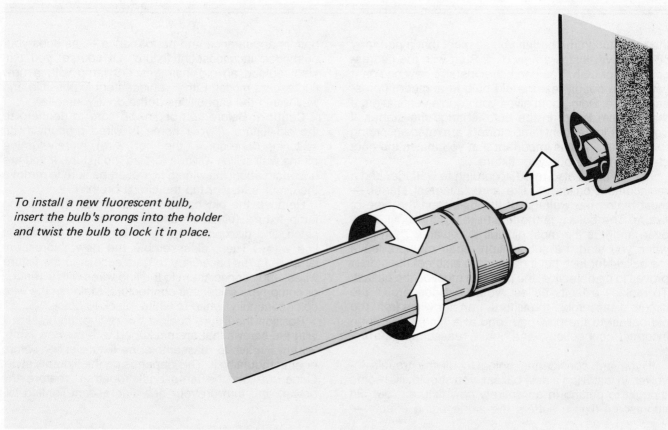

To install a new fluorescent bulb, insert the bulb's prongs into the holder and twist the bulb to lock it in place.

Fluorescent Lamp Trouble-Shooting Chart

PROBLEMS	CAUSES	REPAIRS
Lamp will not light	1. Burned-out bulb.	1. Replace with new fluorescent bulb of correct dimensions and wattage.
	2. Defective starter.	2. Replace starter with new one of appropriate wattage.
	3. Defective ballast, sometimes accompanied by the odor of burning insulation.	3. Consider cost of new ballast in comparison to value of lamp fixture before replacing ballast.
	4. Defective switch.	4. Replace switch.
	5. Lamp not seated correctly in sockets.	5. Reseat lamp in sockets.
	6. No power to lamp.	6. Check power circuit.
Lamp glows dimly	1. Defective bulb.	1. Replace bulb. If lamp has been flashing on and off repeatedly for extended period, starter also should be replaced.
	2. Defective starter.	2. Replace starter with one of correct wattage.
Lamp ends lit	1. Wiring incorrect.	1. Check wiring.
	2. Shorted starter.	2. Replace starter with new one of appropriate wattage.
	3. Bulb burned out.	3. Replace bulb.
Spiraling or flickering lamp	1. Bulb burned out.	1. Replace with new fluorescent bulb of correct dimensions and wattage.
	2. Defective or wrong starter.	2. Replace starter with one of appropriate wattage.
	3. Low line voltage.	3. Check voltage; it must be within 10% of 120 volts.
	4. Wrong ballast.	4. Replace ballast.
Lamp flashes on and off repeatedly	1. Defective bulb.	1. Replace lamp and starter.
	2. Defective starter.	2. Replace starter with one of appropriate wattage.

Caution: Discard old fluorescent lamps carefully. You may already be aware of the possible hazards in throwing away fluorescent bulbs. Youngsters have been injured by glass cuts and chemical effects when they pull discarded bulbs from trash containers. To avoid problems, hide an old bulb at the bottom of the trash or destroy the bulb before you put it in the trash container. Wrap it in heavy paper (a grocery bag is fine), smash the bulb with a hammer, and put the wrapped broken glass in yet another bag before disposing of it properly.

REPLACING A WALL SWITCH

Sometimes, a lamp that is in perfect operating condition does not perform as it should because of a faulty wall switch. There are four primary symptoms of switch failure:

1. When the switch loses its snap, when the handle hangs loosely in any position, or when there is no clear distinction between the "off" and "on" position.

2. When flipping the switch no longer turns the light on or off.

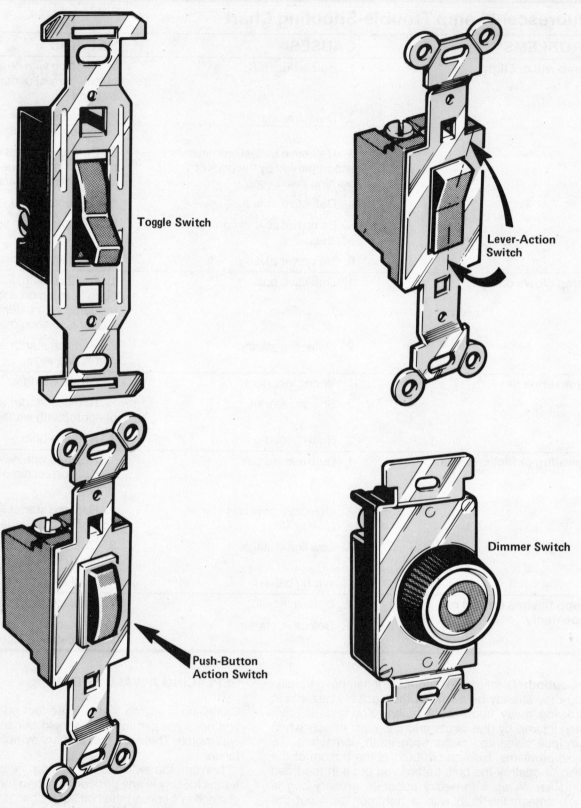

Toggle Switch

Lever-Action Switch

Push-Button Action Switch

Dimmer Switch

There are different types of switches available, but all work on the same general principles. Usually, you can base your selection of a replacement switch on the features you like best.

Here Is What You Will Need

Materials

- Replacement wall switch
- Replacement cover plate (optional)

Tools

- Screwdrivers
- Electrician's diagonal cutters
- Auxiliary light source
- Razor knife (optional)

3. When flipping the switch causes the light to flicker, but not to stay on or off.

4. When the switch may work occasionally, but you must jiggle the handle back and forth several times to keep the light on.

If you spot any of these symptoms of switch failure, install a replacement wall switch as soon as you can.

Caution: First, deenergize the electrical circuit with which you will be working. Then, remove the cover plate. (If the cover plate refuses to come off easily, it is probably being held in place by several layers of paint. Use a razor-blade tool to cut the paint closely around the edge of the plate to free it.) Inspect the old switch to determine the type of replacement model you must buy; but remember that in most instances you can install a better grade of switch than the one you had before. All work on the same general principles, and you can usually base your selection on the features you like best.

The traditional single-pole toggle switch is still the most popular. When the toggle switch is mounted properly, the embossed words "On" and "Off" are upright on the toggle lever, and the light goes on when you flip the switch upward. You can also buy a silent toggle switch. Although it costs more, the silent toggle switch is a pleasure to use and is generally quite durable. One version contains a capsule of mercury that the toggle handle tilts to make electrical contact. It is especially important that you mount such a switch properly; otherwise, the mercury will not make the correct contact.

A variation of the traditional toggle switch is called the lever-action switch. The lever-action switch is designed to lie almost flush with the wall. It turns the fixture on when someone depresses the switch's uppermost part. Another type, the push-button switch, has a single button that turns the light on when pressed, and off when it is pressed again. Push-button switches often feature a built-in neon lamp that glows when the switch is off. The translucent plastic push button allows you to see the glowing lamp, making it easy to locate the switch in the dark. You can install the push-button switch with the built-in glowing lamp as a replacement for nearly any type of switch you presently have in your home.

Some kinds of wall switches have no terminal screws for conductor attachments. Instead, the switch has small holes that are only slightly larger than the bare copper conductors. Once you remove about ½ inch of insulation from the end of the wires, you push the bare ends into the holes. Locking tabs make the electrical connection and grip the wires so that they cannot pull out. To release the wires from the switch, though, all you have to do is insert a narrow-bladed screwdriver in the slot that is right next to the wire-grip holes.

After you decide and purchase the type of replace-

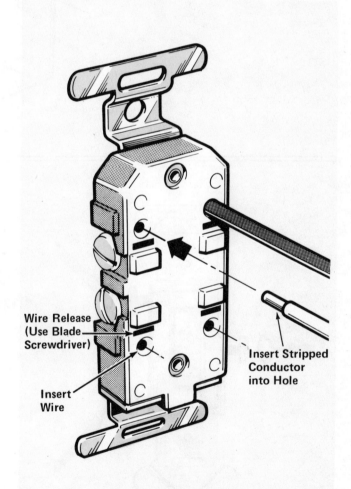

Wire Release (Use Blade Screwdriver)

Insert Wire

Insert Stripped Conductor into Hole

Some switches and receptacles do not have terminal screws for attaching wires; they have only holes into which the stripped ends of wires are inserted to make a secure connection. Other types have both holes and terminal screws, such as the one illustrated.

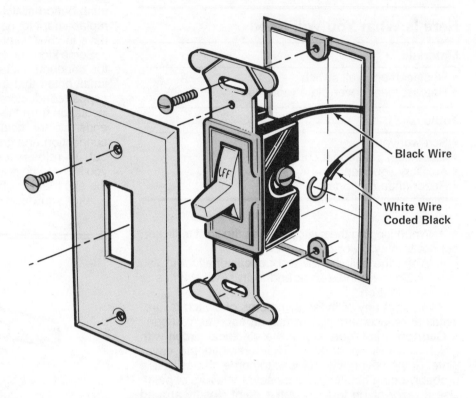

If a switch has only two terminal screws with wires attached, it is a simple on-off (single-pole) switch.

Black Wire

White Wire Coded Black

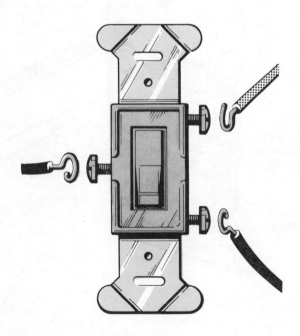

Three-way switches allow you to turn a light on and off from two different locations—such as at the top or at the bottom of a stairway.

ment switch you want to install — and turn off the electric current to the old switch — you are ready to go to work. Remove the mounting screws on the switch cover plate and take off the plate. With the plate removed, you will see two screws holding the switch in the switch box. Remove the screws and carefully pull the switch out of the box as far as the attached wires allow. If there are two screws with wires attached, the switch is a simple on-off (single-pole) type. If there are three screws with wires attached, you are working with a more complicated type called a three-way switch.

Three-way switches allow you to turn a light on and off from two different locations — such as at the top or at the bottom of a stairway. Look carefully at the three terminal screws; you will see that two are one color, while the third is a different color. *Do not* disconnect any wires until you visually compare the old switch with the replacement switch to make sure that you know which wire goes to which terminal screw.

Loosen one of the old terminal screws, remove the wire, and attach the wire to the corresponding terminal screw on the new switch. Then do the same with the remaining wires. Naturally, you should also take care to connect the wires so that all the wire without insulation is safely under the screw heads. Clip off any excess uninsulated wire. The procedure is the same whether you are working with a simple on-off switch or a three-way switch, but you must be more careful with the latter. Verify your wiring by comparing it with the diagram on the box in which your new switch was packaged.

If you are installing the modern wire-grip type of wall switch, cut away the end of each bare wire until only ½ inch of straight length remains. Push one bare end of wire into each wire-grip hole, and check that they have caught properly by tugging gently on them. **Caution:** If the wire insulation, or the conductors, coming into the switch box is brittle or frayed, that part of the circuit or switch loop should be rewired.

Now, the only tasks remaining are to replace the switch in the wall electrical box and install the cover plate. Push the switch into the box carefully, and make sure that the wires fit neatly into the box behind the switch. There are small tabs extending from the switch's mounting bracket; these tabs, called plaster ears, are supposed to lie flat against the wall outside the electrical box. They make certain that the switch stays flush with the wall no matter how the electrical box may be angled inside.

Put the switch back in place, using the two mounting screws that come with the new switch. Oval holes in the mounting bracket allow you to fasten the switch so that it is straight up and down even when the screw holes in the electrical box are tilted. Once you attach the cover plate with the screws you took out earlier — and you replace the circuit fuse or trip the circuit breaker back on — you can enjoy the convenience of a switch that works the way it should.

CHANGING A BROKEN RECEPTACLE

Few people call an electrical convenience outlet by its proper name, a receptacle, but nearly everyone has come across an outlet that does not work as well as it should — or perhaps one that does not work at all. How does it happen that an outlet fails to do its job efficiently and safely? There are two possible explanations.

As you would expect, an electrical convenience outlet can be permanently damaged through improper use. Sticking a hairpin or a paper clip in it, for example, is a sure way to shorten a receptacle's — and your — life. You may never do anything so foolish as sticking hairpins or paper clips in receptacles, but you can do the same damage unwittingly when you plug in an appliance with a short-circuit. No matter how it happens, the damaged receptacle must be replaced.

The other possible explanation for an outlet that fails to do its job efficiently and safely is that it is just so old and has been used so often that it is worn out. There are two clear indications of a worn-out receptacle: The cord drops of its own weight, pulling the plug out from the outlet. Or the plug blades do not make constant electrical contact within the receptacle slots. At that point, the weary old receptacle must be replaced. This is not difficult, but you must follow the correct installation procedures precisely.

Here Is What You Will Need

Materials

- Replacement receptacle (single, duplex or triplex)
- Replacement cover plate (optional)

Tools

- Screwdrivers
- Electrician's diagonal cutters
- Auxiliary light source
- Razor knife (optional)

Inspect your present outlet to see whether it accepts only the plugs with two flat blades or whether it can take a plug that has a round prong (for grounding) in addition to two flat blades. Purchase a new receptacle in a 20-ampere rating that matches the type you are replacing.

After deenergizing the circuit, take off the plate that covers the receptacle. This should be an easy task; the cover plate should fall off when you remove the center screw. The only problem that can occur is when the cover plate is stuck on due to many coats of paint. If you encounter such a problem, cut the paint closely around the edge of the cover plate with a razor knife.

Remove the two screws holding the receptacle in the electrical outlet box and carefully pull the receptacle out of the box as far as the attached line wires allow. Loosen the terminal screws on the receptacle and remove the line wires. **Caution:** If you find that the wiring is quite old and that the insulation is quite brittle, that part of the circuit should be replaced.

Connect the wires to the new receptacle with the

Ungrounded Outlet   **Grounded Outlet**

When replacing a receptacle, see whether it accepts only plugs with two flat blades or whether it can take plugs that have a round ground prong in addition to two flat blades.

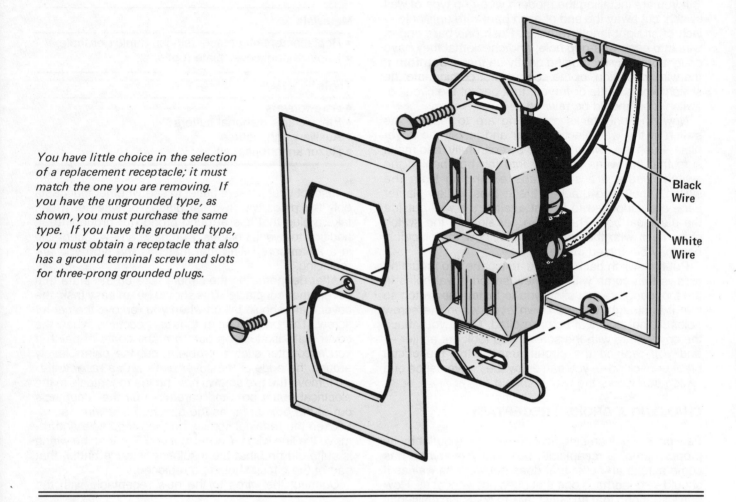

You have little choice in the selection of a replacement receptacle; it must match the one you are removing. If you have the ungrounded type, as shown, you must purchase the same type. If you have the grounded type, you must obtain a receptacle that also has a ground terminal screw and slots for three-prong grounded plugs.

Black Wire

White Wire

white wire under the silver-colored screw and black wire under the dark-colored screw. Fasten the green or bare wire — if present — under the screw with the dab of green color on it and then to the box with a grounding screw or clip. Be sure to loop the line wires in a clockwise direction under the heads of the terminal screws so that as the screw heads are tightened they draw the wire loops in tighter. Naturally, you should also take care to connect the wires so that all the wire without insulation is safely under the screw heads. Clip off any excess uninsulated wire with electrician's diagonal cutters.

Carefully fold the wires into the space in the electrical box behind where the receptacle is to go, and then push the receptacle into the box. Although there is no such thing as "right-side-up" for a two-blade outlet, there is a correct position for outlets designed to handle three-prong grounding plugs. Grounding plugs often attach to their cords at a right angle; and you should

position the receptacle so that the cord will hang down without a loop.

You will also notice that the slots in a receptacle are not identical; one is wider than the other. The wider one connects to the white or neutral wire while the narrower slot connects to the black or "hot" wire. Some plugs, in fact, are designed with one wide and one narrow blade, and they will fit into the receptacle in only one way. The idea behind such a polarized plug is to continue the "hot" and neutral wire identity from the circuit to the appliance.

Once you tighten the two screws that hold the receptacle in the outlet box and you replace the cover plate, your work is done. Restore the fuse or trip the circuit breaker back on.

REPAIRING A BROKEN DOORBELL

A broken doorbell is one of the best examples of an

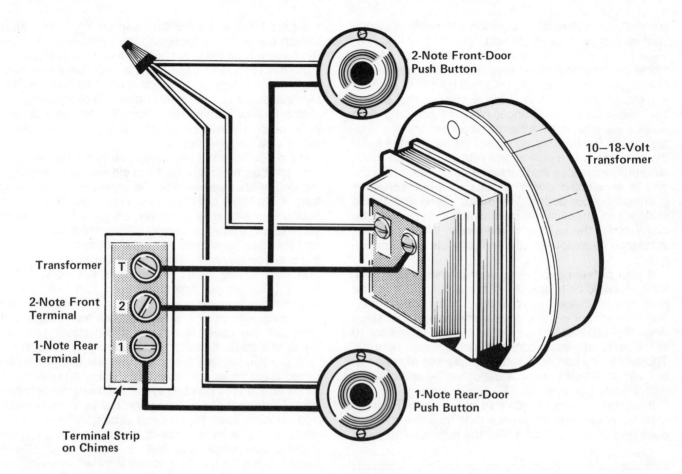

2-Note Front-Door Push Button

10—18-Volt Transformer

Transformer T

2-Note Front Terminal 2

1-Note Rear Terminal 1

Terminal Strip on Chimes

1-Note Rear-Door Push Button

If your doorbell or door chimes do not work, the fault could be in any part of the circuitry—from a push button to the bell or chimes or to the transformer. Before removing any wires at the terminal strip, it is a good idea to tag them so that they can be replaced correctly.

Here Is What You Will Need

Materials

- Replacement door push button (optional)
- 15-volt doorbell or chime set (optional)
- 120- to 15-volt transformer (optional)
- Solderless connectors (optional)

Tools

- Screwdrivers
- Electrician's diagonal cutters
- Wire stripper
- Auxiliary light source
- 12-volt circuit tester (12-volt bulb or bell)
- 110-120-volt circuit tester (if required)
- Continuity tester (optional)

electrical malfunction that many people allow to linger as a continuing annoyance in their homes. It ranks as one of those electrical repairs that many believe requires a professional, and yet one that they know does not need immediate attention. Thus, some homeowners simply put up a sign to tell friends and neighbors that the doorbell does not work, and then settle down to wait until the electrician must be called in for some other pressing task — at which time the doorbell finally gets fixed too.

There is no reason, however, why you must follow this familiar course. Repairing a broken doorbell is certainly a feasible do-it-yourself project, and you can restore your malfunctioning bell — or even install a better bell or chime system — in short time. Some of the newer versions feature a small built-in light bulb that glows through the translucent plastic doorbell button. Such a light makes it easy for visitors to locate your doorbell after dark, and the bulb consumes so little current that its continual operation will make no significant impact on your electric bill.

You can even install a two-tone chime set. Merely follow the mounting instructions on the package. These chimes have two magnetic coils, but both coils perform the same function: They move a plunger that strikes the chime bars. The plunger hits one bar, and then springs back to hit the other bar if necessary (the double tone is for the front door, and the single tone is for the rear door). The only chime sets that operate much differently are those that contain a small motor (like the one in an electric clock). It goes on when someone pushes the door button. The motor opens and closes switches to energize the coils, which then operate the plungers for the various chime tones. When the tone sequence is completed, the motor shuts off automatically.

If your present doorbell or door chimes do not ring, the fault could be in any part of the circuitry — from the push button to the bell or chimes to the transformer. The transformer is the electrical component that steps down the 110-120-volt current to the approximately 10 to 18 volts at which doorbells and chimes operate. Therefore, you can work safely on all parts of the doorbell circuit — except the transformer — without first disconnecting the power.

If you do not know which part of the circuit is faulty, start by removing the screws that hold the doorbell push button to your house. Pull the button as far away

12-Volt
Automobile
Bulb

Socket

A 12-volt automobile lamp socket with two wires makes an effective tester when you are troubleshooting a malfunctioning doorbell or door chimes.

from the building as the circuit wires allow, and then detach the wires by loosening the terminal screws on the button. Now bring the two bare wire ends together. If the bell rings, you know that the fault is in the button. Install a new one by connecting the two wires to the terminal screws of the new button and reattaching the button to your house. The doorbell button is a single-pole switch (two wires attached), and you can place either wire under either screw.

If the bell does not ring when you bring the two bare wire ends together, the fault lies elsewhere — either in the bell or chime assembly, the wiring or in the transformer. Go to the bell or chime and remove the snap-on cover. Removal may, however, be more difficult than you expect. There are several different types of covers, and you may have to try several procedures to remove the one you have. Try lifting the cover upward slightly and then pulling it out. If that does not work, pull it straight out without first lifting it up. Or, look to see whether the snap-on cover is held to the bell or chime assembly with prongs; if so, depress the prongs and then pull the cover to release it. Whatever you do, never pull so hard that you risk damaging the cover.

When you remove the cover, you will see two, three or more terminals and wires, depending on how many tones ring in your doorbell system. If there are only two wires, detach them by loosening the terminal screws, and connect them to a 12-volt circuit tester or attach them to the terminal screws on a substitute bell or chimes. An inexpensive bell or buzzer or a 12-volt automobile lamp bulb in a socket with two wires can be used for testing purposes. If the test bell or buzzer sounds (or the test bulb lights) when you push the doorbell button, you must install a new bell or chime assembly.

If the chime assembly contains three or more wires, tag them in the following manner: "T" (for transformer), "2" (for the two-note front-door chime), and "1" (for the one-note rear-door chime). Loosen the terminal screws, remove all the wires, and connect the wires labeled "T" and "2" to the screw terminals on the substitute test bell. If the test bell rings when you push the front door button, it shows that your old chime set is faulty. To check this conclusion, connect the wires labeled "T" and "1" to the screw terminals on the test bell. If the bell rings when you push the rear door button, then you are doubly certain that you must replace the chimes.

What do you do when you find that neither the button nor the bell is defective? By process of elimination, you now know that the problem must be in the transformer or the wiring. You will usually find the transformer mounted on an electrical junction box, subpanel or main entrance panel. Generally, the transformer connections to the power lines are hidden from view within the box. The bell wires are attached to exposed terminal screws on the transformer. Connect the test bell directly to the low-voltage (exposed) transformer terminals. If the bell does not ring, then you can be sure that the transformer is defective or not getting power.

Caution: Unlike the other parts of the doorbell circuit, the transformer primary, or 110-120-volt input, carries current that can threaten your safety. Therefore, you *must* deenergize the branch circuit that supplies power to the transformer. Remove the appropriate fuse, trip the correct circuit breaker or throw the main switch to shut off all the electricity in your home (necessary only when you do not know which fuse to pull or circuit breaker to trip).

Before replacing the transformer, check to make sure that it indeed is getting power from the 110-120-volt circuit. With the circuit deenergized, disconnect the transformer from the line wires. One easy way to make a line circuit test is to attach a spare screw-terminal lamp socket, fitted with a 110-120-volt bulb, to the line wires. If the terminals are exposed, wrap a length of electrical tape around the socket to cover them. You can also use an old lamp; remove the plug, and connect the lamp wires to the line wires with wirenuts. Then turn the circuit back on again. If the lamp lights, the circuit is fine and the transformer is not; replace it.

An alternative and easier method of testing, if you are sure of your skills as a home electrician, is to separate the two line wires so that they *cannot* touch each other or any part of the electrical box. Turn the circuit back on, and gently touch the probes of a 110-120-volt circuit tester to the bare wire ends. If you get a positive indication from the tester (tester light glows, or indicator reads 110-120 volts), the circuit is alright. **Caution:** Always keep in mind that you are working with "hot" wires; so do not touch them!

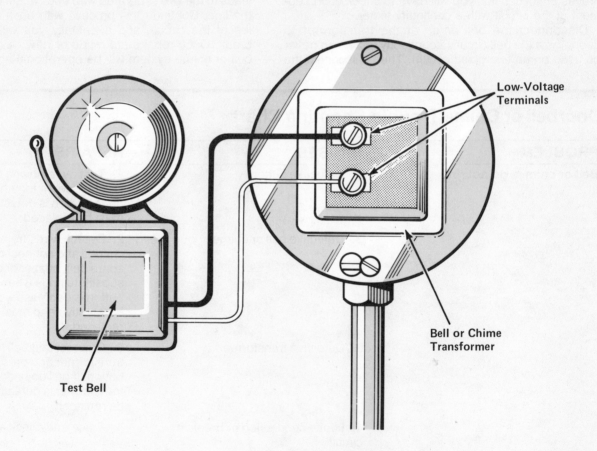

Low-Voltage Terminals

Bell or Chime Transformer

Test Bell

To check the transformer, connect a test bell to the transformer's low-voltage (exposed) terminals. If the test bell does not ring, you can be sure that the transformer is defective or is not getting power.

If the transformer is defective, deenergize the circuit and remove the transformer. Buy a replacement model of the same voltage and wattage (or VA — volt/amps). You can find the electrical information stamped on the transformer, and you should find installation instructions on the package. Follow the instructions carefully, and use crimp-on connectors or wirenuts to attach the new transformer to the circuit line wires of your electrical system. Then connect the bell wires to the low-voltage screw terminals on the transformer, turn the power back on, and press the doorbell button. If you installed the transformer properly, you should once again hear your home's bell or chime assembly sound as it should.

If the transformer and its power circuit prove to be alright, the only possibility left is a break or loose connection somewhere in the bell wiring. Since the latter is the more likely possibility, trace the entire bell circuit from transformer to bell or chimes to push buttons, and search for a loose terminal screw or wire joint. If this proves unsuccessful, you will have to check each segment of the circuit with a continuity tester.

Disconnect the bell wires at the transformer to deenergize the bell circuit (a continuity tester can never be used on an energized circuit). Then disconnect the transformer wires at the bell or chimes, and twist them together just enough so that they make good contact with one another. Go back to the transformer, and touch the probe leads of the continuity tester to the bare ends of the bell wires. If the tester lights up, or you get a reading on the meter dial, the circuit has continuity and there are no breaks or loose connections in the line; that part of the circuit is alright. If the tester does not register, there is a break somewhere.

If there is a break, you must try to locate it and make repairs. Sometimes, however, especially where much of the bell circuit wiring is hidden within walls or is otherwise inaccessible, the easiest course is to run a new segment of bell wire along whatever path is easiest, and forget about the old wiring segment.

If that particular segment of the bell circuit proves to be fault-free, you must go on to the next segment and check it in the same manner. Make sure that both ends of the segment are disconnected; twist the two wires together at one end of the line and touch the tester leads to the two separated wire ends at the other end of the line. Continue this process with each segment or leg of the circuit, and eventually you will locate the break. Once repairs are made or new wire is run, the bell or chime system will be operational again.

Doorbell or Chime Trouble-Shooting Chart

PROBLEM	CAUSES	REPAIRS
Bell or chimes do not ring	1. Defective button.	1. Test by removing button and touching wires together. If bell rings, button is defective and must be replaced.
	2. Defective bell or chimes.	2. Detach wires from bell or chimes and connect them to a spare bell, buzzer or chime. If substitute rings when doorbell button is depressed, present bell is defective and must be replaced.
	3. Defective transformer.	3. Connect test bell to transformer and press door button. If bell does not ring, transformer is defective and must be replaced.
	4. Loose connection or break in circuit.	4. Trace and check all wiring.
	5. No power at transformer.	5. Check to see that circuit is turned on; check for loose connection at transformer primary. If transformer is defective, it must be replaced.

New Installations

It is one thing to repair or replace malfunctioning components in your home's electrical system and quite another to install entirely new components. It is, for example, a relatively simple task to hang a new lighting fixture in the same electrical box that served a previous fixture, but it is a bit more complicated when you want to add fixtures to a ceiling or wall that previously had no fixtures whatsoever. Nonetheless, you can handle these installations yourself — with no danger to your safety and with a substantial savings over what it would cost to have the same job performed by a professional electrician.

Moreover, the new installations you can do yourself are not limited to lighting fixtures. You can add several types of switches — dimmer, three-way, and pilot light — and three kinds of receptacles: general-purpose, clock, and 220-240-volt versions. In addition, outdoor fixtures, permanent timer devices, and new circuits and circuit breakers are all within the capabilities of the well-informed do-it-yourselfer. In other words, you can do much more than merely fix the breakdowns in your electrical system or replace worn-out components; you can actually remodel your electrical system to provide new convenience and beauty in your home.

NEW LIGHTING FIXTURES

There is nothing terribly complicated about installing a new lighting fixture, but the job does require some planning in advance. Naturally, work is much simpler when you can install the fixture in a room that is not yet totally constructed; that is, before the plaster or the drywall is up. You can put a new fixture in a finished room, but in such cases you must cut into the walls to install the wiring and electrical boxes.

You may already know exactly where you want to locate the new lighting fixture and the new wall switch, but there are some other considerations to keep in mind. For the most uniform light throughout the room, put the fixture in the exact center of the ceiling; on the other hand, place the lighting directly over a table or desk if that is where it is needed most. There is no limitation on where you should locate a new lighting fixture, but some point between ceiling joists is often easiest. Of course, you are not limited to the ceiling as the place for your new fixture; put it on a wall if that better suits your decorating motif.

Switch location is more a matter of practicality than aesthetics. Most people, when entering a darkened room, reach to their right to find the light switch. Therefore, your new switch should be to the right of the entry door and about 4½ feet above the floor. If possible, install the electrical box that holds the switch alongside a wall stud; the stud provides a secure point of attachment. You can, however, install the switch elsewhere if you use the kind of box that has a flare clamp to hold it

Here Is What You Will Need

Materials

- 2″ x 3″ switch box with cover plate
- Single-pole toggle switch
- 4″ octagonal box(es) (one for each fixture)
- Lighting fixture(s)
- Length of Type NM #12-2 or #14-2 cable with ground (or other cable, as required)
- Staples for Type NM cable (or other, as required)
- Solderless connectors (wirenuts)
- Miscellaneous hardware
- Box mounting hangers
- Scrap bare copper wire
- Electrical tape (optional)

Tools

- Marking pencil
- Screwdrivers
- Electrician's diagonal cutters
- Drill with bits
- Keyhole or saber saw
- Auxiliary light source (optional)
- Stepladder (optional)
- Tape measure
- Hammer
- Punch (optional)
- Fish-wire or snake (optional)
- Wire stripper
- Pliers (optional)
- Utility knife
- Scratch awl (optional)
- Armored cable cutter (optional)

against wallboard or if you secure a standard box with a pair of plaster clips.

In describing the installation procedures for a new lighting fixture, we will assume that you want the light fixture in the ceiling of the room and that you will use Type NM nonmetallic sheathed cable for the project. The new wiring will go through the attic (to the fixture), the basement (to the main entrance panel), and the walls. Therefore, buy enough Type NM cable — the kind that contains two #12 or #14 insulated conductors and one bare conductor (the conductor size is stamped on the cable) — to run from the main entrance panel to the fixture and switch, with a 6- to 8-inch length of cable inside each electrical box. Since you will do everything else before you connect the cable to the electrical system, you need not disconnect any circuits

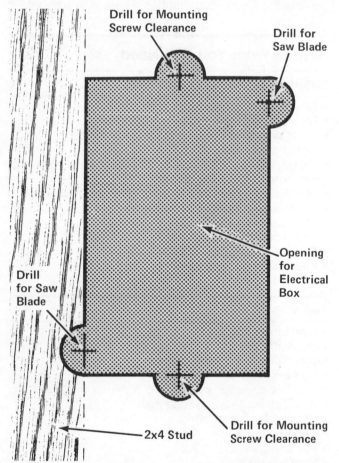

Electrical wall boxes may be installed alongside or between wall studs. If you plan to install a box next to a stud, this actual-size template can be used for some types of standard electrical boxes. It indicates four points for drilling holes into a wall, so that a saw blade can be inserted to cut the box opening and so that there will be clearance for the mounting screws.

until you reach the final procedures.

Place an electrical switch box — open end facing the plaster or drywall — at the wall location that you selected for the switch. Draw a pencil line around the box as you hold it against the wall; but be sure, as you draw the outline, not to include the plaster ears of the electrical box. Then turn the box so that the open end faces you, and refine your outline to include the corner projections on the box. Follow the same procedure to outline a 4-inch octagonal box on the ceiling at the fixture location.

The outlined areas must now be cut out of the wall and ceiling. Drill ⅜-inch holes through the plaster or drywall at the corners of your outline into the hollow part of the wall. Drill the holes so that the edges will take care of the corner projections on the electrical box. Now, starting at the drilled holes, cut away the plaster or drywall along the lines of your outline, using a keyhole or saber saw. Cut out the electrical box areas for the wall switch and for as many ceiling fixtures as you plan to install.

Next, mount the box for the ceiling fixture (do not mount the wall switch box until later). You will need a hanger bracket to mount the ceiling box, and you can choose whatever type of bracket works best from the many types of box hangers that are available.

Carefully measure below the floor and above the ceiling to determine the points directly below and above the wall switch. While you are in the attic, drill a ⅝-inch hole through the floor so that you enter the wall cavity at a point directly above the wall switch; and, while you are in the basement, drill a ⅝-inch hole through the ceiling so that you enter the wall cavity at a point directly below the wall switch. Drop a string weighted with a nut or bolt from the attic floor hole, and retrieve the string at the large hole you cut earlier for the wall switch electrical box.

Once you get to this point, you need someone else to help you for the next few steps. The other person should go up to the attic. Remove the weight from the string and attach Type NM cable to the string at the wall switch hole. Bare the conductor ends of the cable, bend them in a loop, tie the string to the loop, and cover the joint with tape to make it smooth enough to go through the hole in the attic floor without snagging.

Feed the string and cable up into the hollow wall space through the wall switch hole as your assistant pulls them up through the hole in the attic floor. The string is a big help in getting the cable up through the wall space, but you and your helper must be careful. Do not rely primarily on the string; instead, push the cable to feed it up to the attic. Pulling hard on the string is a sure way to separate it from the cable. Have your assistant pull through enough cable to reach the ceiling fixture box, with an additional 6 to 8 inches for installing the cable inside it. Once the cable passes through the hole in the attic floor, of course, your helper can re-

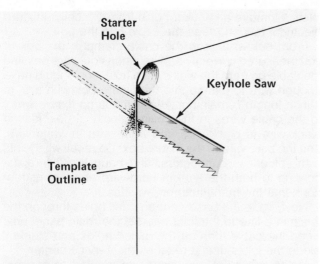

After drilling holes in the wall for an electrical box, the blade of a keyhole saw or saber saw can be inserted to cut the opening.

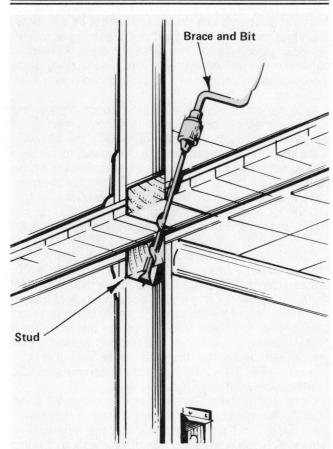

To route cable between the switch box and the ceiling fixture, drill a hole through the attic floor so that you enter the wall cavity at a point directly above the wall switch opening.

move the string and work with the cable itself.

From your position at the switch box hole, cut the cable where it enters the wall, but allow 6 to 8 inches extra for the wall switch electrical box that you will install later. Then have your assistant push a stiff wire up from the basement through the ceiling hole to where you can reach it through the switch box hole. You can then use the wire to pull the cable upward. Once your helper attaches the Type NM cable to the wire in the basement, pull it toward the switch box hole. But again, you should not rely so much on pulling the wire as on someone pushing the cable up from below. Feed the cable up the wall and out through the switch hole about 6 to 8 inches. Have your assistant take the other end of the cable to the main panel. There should be 6 to 8 inches extra on the cable length to allow for connections at the main panel. NOTE: Sometimes, with luck, you can feed the Type NM cable itself down from the attic and up from the basement without resorting to strings and fish-wires — this is always worth a try.

With the cable in position at the switch box hole — one end leading up to the fixture box in the attic floor and the other end going down to the main panel in the basement — you are ready to install the cable in the electrical boxes. Remove one knockout disc from each end of the switch box, feed in the two cable ends, and fasten the cables with the clamps in the switch box. Push the box into the hole you cut earlier, and fasten it to the wall stud with nails or screws through the holes in the side of the box; make sure, however, that the front edge of the box is flush with the surface of the wall before you fasten it. If your walls are lath and plaster or wood instead of drywall, you can use the plaster ears to attach the box to the wall.

Now come the all-important electrical connections; be sure to follow directions carefully. Slit the outer cover of each cable end inside the electrical box, peel the cover back, and cut it off. Then, remove the last inch of insulation from the ends of the black and white wires. The best way to remove the insulation without nicking the conductors is to use a wire stripper; be sure to select the right cutting slots in the stripper jaws for the size of conductors.

Twist the white wires from each cable together firmly and attach a wirenut to cover the joint. Twist the two bare wires and the end of a length of scrap bare copper wire together and attach a wirenut. Secure the other end of the scrap bare copper wire to the switch box with a grounding clip or screw. Loop one black wire under each of the two screws on the switch, and tighten the screws. Be sure to loop the wires in a clockwise direction under the heads of the terminal screws so that as the screw heads are tightened they draw the wire loops in tighter. You should also take care to connect the wires so that all the wire without insulation is safely under the screw heads. Clip off any excess uninsulated wire with diagonal cutters. Switching is always done in

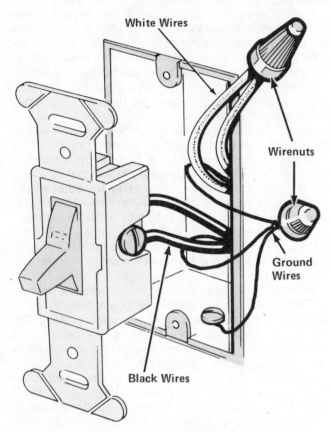

White Wires

Wirenuts

Ground
Wires

Black Wires

At the wall switch, connect the two black wires to the switch, and join the two white wires with a wirenut. Twist one end of a length of scrap copper wire together with the ends of the two bare ground wires and join them with a wirenut. Secure the other end of the scrap wire to the switch box with a grounding clip or screw.

joists. Remove a knockout disc from the ceiling fixture electrical box and feed the cable into the box.

From below, tighten the cable clamp in the box. If you measured correctly earlier, when you were passing the cable up from the wall switch hole, you should have enough wire to extend into the fixture box with a 6- to 8-inch length remaining. Attach the lamp fixture wires to the cable wires in the ceiling electrical box, joining black wire to black wire and white wire to white wire, and the bare wire to the fixture box. Cover all wire joints with solderless connectors, and hang the fixture according to both the type of hardware and the instructions that the manufacturer provides.

Now, go to the basement and drill holes through the joists in a line to the joist nearest the main panel box. Feed the cable through the drilled holes and staple it along the joists until it reaches the service center.

Up to this point, you have not needed to concern yourself about the dangers of live current, but now you must be careful. Turn off the main circuit breaker — or pull the main fuses — to disconnect all the circuits in your home from the incoming power lines. You will need an auxiliary light source now because all the circuits in your home are dead. That is not to say, however, that you have eliminated any possibility of receiving a dangerous shock. The wires at the top of the main panel box are still energized. Remove the cover from the box, but be very careful to avoid those power lines at the top.

With the cover off, tap a tapered punch against the side of a knockout disc to start its removal; then finish the job with pliers to break the disc out of the box wall. Naturally, the knockout disc you choose to remove should be the one most conveniently located to where your cable run ends. Fasten a cable clamp in the hole, pass the cable through, and tighten the clamp.

Look for a spare circuit in the box, but if you cannot find a spare, select the most lightly loaded circuit for your new lighting fixture.

Correlate the wire conductor size to the circuit breaker or fuse rating: #12 to either a 15- or a 20-ampere rating, #14 only to a 15-ampere rating. Strip off the outer cable cover, remove about ½ inch of insulation from each of the conductors, and slide the straight bare end of the black wire under the terminal screw (not under the screw head) that is alongside the circuit you selected. Fasten the white wire and the bare ground wire in the same way under separate available terminal screws on the ground bus.

Once you place the cover back on the main panel box, trip the main circuit breaker back on or restore the main fuses, and place light bulbs in the new lighting fixture. You can enjoy the result of your work by flipping the wall switch. It may have taken you a bit of time and a little labor, but you know that the job was done right and at a fraction of the cost that a professional electrician would charge for the same installation.

the black or "hot" wire, never in the white (or neutral) wire; therefore, the black wires and not the white ones go to the screws on the switch. When you complete all the electrical connections, mount the wall switch in the electrical box and attach the cover plate.

Next, go to the attic and drill holes through the joists in a line from where the cable enters the attic floor to the joist nearest the ceiling fixture. The holes should be in the center of each joist to keep the cable down far enough to prevent anything from hitting it. Feed the cable through the drilled holes. If you come to a point where the cable runs alongside the joist instead of through it, make a loop — not a sharp bend — in the cable to alter its direction and staple it where necessary. Feed the cable through and along the joists until it reaches the fixture box. Staple the cable to the joist within 12 inches of the end of the run; no staples are required when the cable runs through holes drilled in

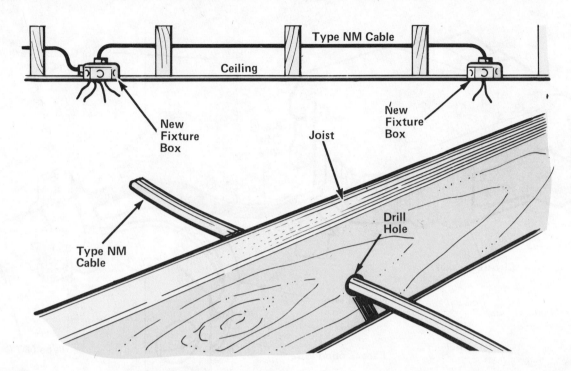

Type NM Cable

Ceiling

New
Fixture
Box

New
Fixture
Box

Joist

Type NM
Cable

Drill
Hole

Electrical cable may be run through ceiling joists. The holes for the cable should be drilled in the center of the joists to keep the cable down far enough to prevent anything from hitting it.

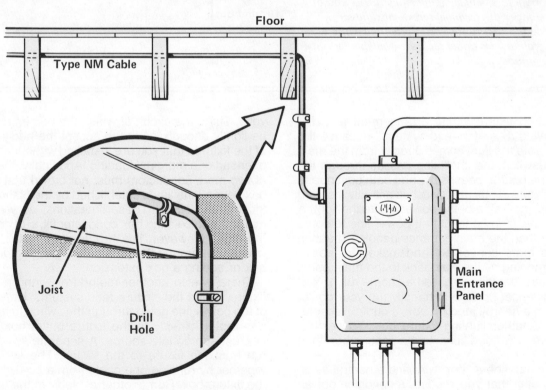

Floor

Type NM Cable

Joist

Drill
Hole

Main
Entrance
Panel

The cable must also run to the main entrance panel. Again, it may be run through joists. Where cable runs alongside a joist instead of through it, staple or clamp it where necessary.

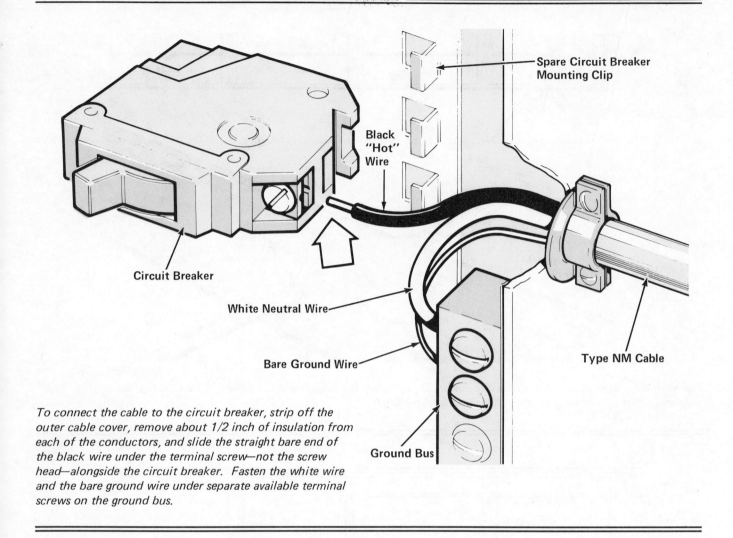

Spare Circuit Breaker Mounting Clip

Black "Hot" Wire

Circuit Breaker

White Neutral Wire

Bare Ground Wire

Type NM Cable

Ground Bus

To connect the cable to the circuit breaker, strip off the outer cable cover, remove about 1/2 inch of insulation from each of the conductors, and slide the straight bare end of the black wire under the terminal screw—not the screw head—alongside the circuit breaker. Fasten the white wire and the bare ground wire under separate available terminal screws on the ground bus.

The switched fixture wiring arrangement just discussed is called a "switch-feed system," because the power to operate the light comes directly from the main panel to the switch, the "hot" line passes through the switch and the neutral passes by, and both continue to the lighting fixture. Thus, the switch is actually inserted directly in the "hot" side of the power line to the light. A variation on this is to connect that power line to some source other than the main entrance panel, a situation that often is more convenient and makes for easier wiring than running all the way back to the main panel (such a line, incidentally, is called a "home run"). You might, for instance, be able to handily run your power feed line from a nearby junction box, a duplex receptacle or even another lighting fixture box. To do this, though, there are conditions to be met, other than ready access.

First, there must be a "hot" wire and a neutral available in the outlet that you choose, a condition not always true of fixture or even junction boxes. Second, the power source in the box must be, of course, 110-120

volts. Third, the circuit of which the box is a part must be lightly enough loaded to accept the additional load of the fixtures that you are installing without causing an overload or a marginal loading. And finally, the addition of two more conductors must not crowd that electrical box beyond the limits established by the National Electrical Code (NEC). These limitations, as well as formulae for calculating box conductor fill, can be found in the NEC. However, if a box is already full, you can usually get around the problem by ganging on another box or adding a box extension.

There is also another method of wiring a switched fixture, called the "fixture-feed system." Here, instead of the power line going through the switch to the fixture, it is routed directly to the fixture outlet box from the nearest appropriate source. A separate switch loop is run from the fixture to the switch. The system goes together by running one cable from a power source to the fixture box. Run another cable from the fixture box to the switch box. Connect the black wire to one side of the switch and the bare equipment-grounding conductor to the switch box with a grounding screw or clip. With an indelible felt-tip pen, paint the white conductor black, and attach it to the other switch terminal. At the fixture box, connect the black line wire to the black switch-loop wire with a solderless connector, and attach the bare equipment-grounding conductors to the fixture box. Connect the white line wire to the white fixture wire with a solderless connector. Color the white switch-loop wire black, and connect it to the black fixture wire. Other parts of the lighting fixture installation are done in the same way as previously explained.

OUTDOOR LIGHTING

Installing lighting fixtures outside your house is no more difficult than putting new fixtures in a ceiling inside; the major difference, in fact, is in the materials you must use for outdoor wiring. The nonmetallic sheathed cable that you ran from attic to basement during the installation of a new ceiling fixture is not suitable or approved for outdoor use. Instead, you need a special type of cable, called Type UF, which is designed for burial in the ground. Its tough plastic outer sheath can withstand nearly all environmental conditions except exposure to sunlight.

Once you obtain the materials required for an outdoor lighting installation, an enormous array of creative possibilities opens up to you. It is fair to say that of all the different new installations a do-it-yourselfer can tackle, outside lighting provides the best opportunity to exercise imagination and ingenuity. You can light a walkway, outline a driveway, spotlight a garden, and create many more interesting effects that involve the dramatic impact of a pool of light in the midst of surrounding darkness.

Suppose, for example, that you want to install an escort light alongside a sidewalk. You must run wiring from the main entrance panel (or some other appropriate source) through the wall of your home, to an outside weatherproof electrical box and switch. From the switch, you run Type UF cable to the fixture. You must bury the cable in a trench to a depth of not less than 12 inches, but you *never* place electrical boxes underground where they would be totally inaccessible. To protect the cable — as well as to support the fixture — you run the cable through rigid conduit or EMT (electrical metallic tubing) at the points where it enters and leaves the ground; galvanized steel conduit is most commonly used, but EMT, aluminum or even plastic conduit are other possibilities; be guided by locally approved practices. Since you make all the new circuit wiring connections first — leaving the connections to the electrical system until the end — you need not concern yourself about live circuits until you have nearly completed the installation.

The first thing to do is to measure the length of cable you need, which may not be as easy as it sounds.

Here Is What You Will Need

Materials

- Length of Type UF #12-2 or #14-2 cable with ground wire
- Lengths of Type NM #12-2 or #14-2 cable with ground wire (or other cable, as required)
- Weatherproof switch box(es) with cover plates
- Right-angle conduit outlet(s)
- Outside fixture(s)
- 4″ octagonal junction box(es) with blank cover(s)
- Lengths of ½″ rigid conduit or EMT
- Single-pole toggle switch(es)
- ½″ rigid conduit or EMT clamps
- Type NM cable staples (or other, as required)
- ½″ insulating bushings
- ½″ cable clamps
- ½″ locknuts
- Solderless connectors
- GFI circuit breaker
- Miscellaneous hardware
- Electrical tape (optional)
- Elastomeric caulking compound

Tools

- Screwdrivers
- Electrician's diagonal cutters
- Pipe cutter and threading dies (optional)
- Pick axe (optional)
- Spade
- Sod cutter (optional)
- Adjustable wrench (optional)
- Wire stripper
- Drill with bits
- Tape measure
- Marking pencil
- Punch (optional)
- Pliers (optional)
- Hacksaw (optional)
- Scratch awl (optional)
- Armored cable cutter (optional)
- Tube bender

Measure the distance from the power source inside your home to the lamp socket in the outdoor fixture, but add on enough to allow for the fact that wiring never can match the "shortest-distance" path that your tape measure followed. Were you to purchase a length of cable that is just barely sufficient, you might find yourself with a short piece of cable to work with in the electrical box — an exasperating if not impossible situation. Buy as much Type UF and Type NM #12-2 w/g or #14-2 w/g cable ("w/g" indicates "with bare ground wire") as your outdoor lighting situation requires.

Next, drill a ⅞-inch hole from the inside of your home

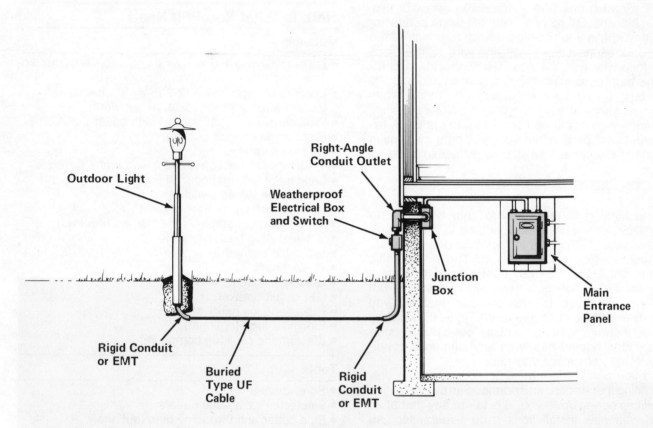

Outdoor Light

Right-Angle Conduit Outlet

Weatherproof Electrical Box and Switch

Junction Box

Main Entrance Panel

Rigid Conduit or EMT

Buried Type UF Cable

Rigid Conduit or EMT

To install an escort light alongside a walkway, you must run cable from the main entrance panel or other suitable circuit, through an outside wall of your home, to an outside weatherproof electrical box and switch, and finally to the lighting fixture itself.

to the outside. Usually, the best location for the hole — through which cable will run — is at or immediately above the wood plate of the house foundation. Should you find masonry (bricks, concrete, stucco or concrete blocks) at your chosen location, however, you must use a suitable masonry drill for making the hole.

Now you must dig a narrow trench at least 12 inches deep from the planned location of the escort light in your yard all the way to a point immediately below the hole in the wall of your home. You can lay the Type UF cable in the trench, but do not bury it yet. You will have to maneuver the cable a bit before you can bury it permanently in the ground.

Go back to the point in the wall where you drilled the hole and assemble the following electrical parts: a length of rigid (or other) conduit calculated to reach from the base of the trench to the hole in the wall, a weatherproof electrical switch box, a close nipple, a right-angle conduit outlet, and a piece of conduit to go through the wall. The opening in the conduit outlet should face the same way as the open end of the

weatherproof box. Feed the end of the Type UF cable from the trench, up through the conduit, and into the weatherproof box — leaving a 6-inch length of cable in the box. Position the assembled electrical parts so that the horizontal conduit runs through the hole in the wall and the vertical conduit runs down into the trench, but avoid making a sharp bend in the cable where it leaves the conduit to run through the trench. Good scuff protection can be gained here by bending the end of the conduit in the trench and threading a plastic insulating bushing onto the end of the conduit.

Before you can do any more work outside, you must go inside to the hole you drilled earlier. Affix a 4-inch octagonal box or a conduit outlet to the end of the through-the-hole conduit. If you are using an octagonal box, remove a ½-inch knockout disc in the bottom of the box, thread a ½-inch locknut in all the way on the threaded end of the conduit, put the box on through its knockout, and tighten another ½-inch locknut on the threaded conduit inside the box. You may need to add some kind of spacer (like a piece of plywood) behind the octagonal box to allow you to fasten it to the wall.

Go back outside again, and affix the electrical parts — including the weatherproof box — to the wall. Use conduit clamps to secure the parts, placing one clamp immediately below the box. Next screw a section of conduit to the fixture itself to support it. It should be long enough to extend from the trench bottom to a suitable height aboveground for the fixture. Bend the end of the conduit at the base of the trench and thread a plastic insulating bushing onto the end of the conduit.

With the conduit screwed on at one end, disassemble the outdoor lighting fixture enough so that you can get to the terminal screws on the lamp socket. Run the end of the Type UF cable through the conduit and up to the socket, allowing sufficient cable length so that you can bare the wire ends and attach them to the terminal screws. Secure the bare grounding wire to some convenient part of the fixture with a grounding clip or screw. After you complete the cable connections, reassemble the fixture, place it in its intended location with the end of the conduit at the bottom of the trench (being careful not to put a sharp bend in the cable), and fill in the trench.

Go back to the house wall and remove the cover plate from the right-angle conduit outlet. Run a length of Type NM cable (the same size as the Type UF) from inside the house, through the conduit in the wall and the conduit outlet, and down into the weatherproof box. Replace the conduit outlet cover plate once you maneuver the cable into the box. Bare the ends of the two cables in the weatherproof box and join white wire to white wire with a solderless connector. Connect the two black wires to the terminal screws of a single-pole toggle switch; such a switch allows you to turn the escort light on and off from the outside. Join the two bare wires with a solderless connector, and mount the weatherproof switch cover on the box.

Make one more trip to the basement, and run a length of Type NM cable from the main entrance panel or some other nearby power source to the octagonal box. Strip the two cables in the box and connect the wires — black to black, white to white, and bare ground to bare ground. The ground circuit should also be attached to the box with a grounding clip or screw. After deenergizing the main panel, attach the other end of the black wire of the Type NM cable to a spare or lightly loaded circuit in the main panel. **Caution:** The incoming power lines at the top of your main entrance panel are still energized. NOTE: An outdoor lighting circuit should be connected to a ground fault circuit interrupter (GFI) type of circuit breaker in the interest of safety. If an outdoor receptacle is included in the circuit, whether separate or as a part of an outdoor lighting fixture, the circuit *must,* according to the NEC, be connected to a GFI.

Remove the cover from the main panel box. Tap a punch against the side of a knockout disc to start its removal; then finish the job with pliers to break the disc out of the box wall. The disc you remove should be one conveniently located to the circuit breaker you will be using. Fasten a cable clamp in the hole, pass the cable through, and tighten the clamp. Strip off the cable cover, remove about ½ inch of insulation from each of the conductors, and slide the straight bare end of the black wire under the terminal screw (not under the screw head) that is alongside the circuit you selected. Fasten the white wire and the bare ground wire in the same way under separate available terminal screws on the ground bus. Place the cover back on the main panel box.

Finally, put a blank cover plate on the octagonal box, and turn the power back on. Creating outdoor lighting effects may seem like a great deal of work, but once you flip that fixture switch, you will see how worthwhile all your effort has been.

There are circumstances where having the outdoor light control switch indoors, perhaps near a patio or front door, is more desirable than mounting the switch outdoors. In many respects, this makes for an easier installation, too. The trench is dug and the fixture installed just as previously discussed. But to carry the cable inside, all you have to do is bore a ¾-inch hole through your house foundation and into the cellar or crawl space at about the same level as the trench bottom. Run the Type UF cable inside and directly into an octagonal junction box mounted at any nearby spot. Seal the hole through the foundation with an elastomeric caulking compound both inside and outside, and fill the trench. Then run a line of Type NM cable from the octagonal box to a conveniently located switch box, and from the switch box to a power source, just as though you were wiring up an indoor lighting fixture. Make the connections at the junction box by joining the conductors color to color with solderless connectors and attaching the joined bare conductors to the box. The switch and power connections are made in the usual fashion.

INSTALLING NEW TYPES OF SWITCHES

You have seen how to install the on-off switch that must accompany the installation of a new lighting fixture, but that represents only a fraction of what the do-it-yourselfer can do with electrical switches. You can install a separate switch for the same fixture at another location; you can put in a switch that allows you to dim or brighten an incandescent fixture gradually; you can add a lighted reminder switch that tells you when lights are on in an area you have overlooked; and, finally, you can install a permanent timer switch that automatically turns electrical devices on and off at preset intervals. All of these installations can make your home more convenient, more enjoyable, and more valuable. Best of all, you can do them yourself and save money.

Adding a Three-Way Switch

There must be at least one light in your home that you would like to be able to switch on and off from more than one location. What about the light at the top of the stairway that you would like to turn on before you go upstairs? Similarly, think how convenient it would be to control a lighting fixture from either end of a long hallway. These are just typical examples that can be found in nearly any home; undoubtedly, there is a specific situation in your home where a three-way switch would be a tremendous convenience.

If you decide to add a second switch, however, not only must it be a three-way device, but you must also convert the present on-off switch to a three-way switch. The three-way switch is so named because it has three wires connected to it — the ordinary on-off switch has just two wire connections. Naturally, you must connect the two switches to each other with three-wire cable. Therefore, to switch the lamp on and off from two places, you must install another electrical box, run three-conductor cable between the two boxes, install a three-way switch in the new box, and change the existing on-off switch to a three-way switch. All of this sounds much more complicated than it really is.

Take a look at a three-way switch and you will see

that there are three terminal screws — two are alike, while the third is different in some way (that is, color, shape or location). The outside terminal on many three-way switches is the different one, and the facing-in terminals are the similar ones. If you were to cross the wires going to the two similar terminals, the switch would still work.

You must, of course, decide where you want to locate the second three-way switch. Naturally, you want it in the most convenient location, and you can select a spot where you can fasten the switch box to a wall stud, either exposed or behind the wall, or between studs for plaster-clip mounting. Measure the length of cable you will need to run from the existing switch box to the proposed location of the new switch box, and be sure to allow for the additional length (6 to 8 inches) that you will need inside each box. Once you know how much cable you will need, purchase the right amount of Type NM three-wire cable; the kind you need contains three #14 (15-ampere circuit) or three #12 (15- or 20-ampere circuit) insulated conductors (the conductor size is marked on the cover of the cable) and one bare wire.

If your new three-way switch is going to be surface-mounted on a wall or post, obtain the kind of switch box that is called a "handy" box. Attach a suitable length of

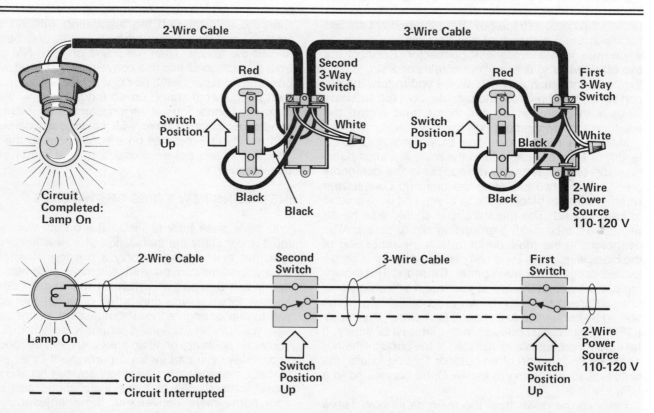

The illustrations and accompanying diagrams above and on page 55 depict how a pair of three-way switches can control a light fixture at the end of a run—if the power goes to the first switch.

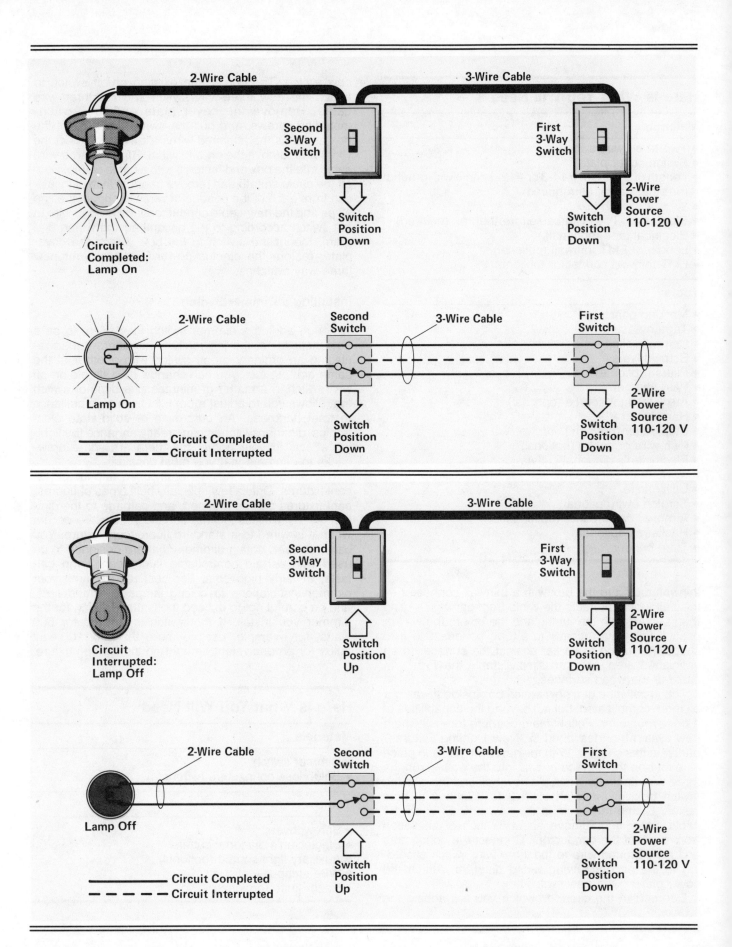

2-Wire Cable   **3-Wire Cable**

Second
3-Way
Switch

First
3-Way
Switch

Switch
Position
Down

Switch
Position
Down

2-Wire
Power
Source
110-120 V

Circuit
Completed:
Lamp On

2-Wire Cable   Second
Switch   **3-Wire Cable**   First
Switch

Lamp On

Switch
Position
Down

Switch
Position
Down

2-Wire
Power
Source
110-120 V

——————— Circuit Completed
— — — — — Circuit Interrupted

2-Wire Cable   **3-Wire Cable**

Second
3-Way
Switch

First
3-Way
Switch

Switch
Position
Up

Switch
Position
Down

2-Wire
Power
Source
110-120 V

Circuit
Interrupted:
Lamp Off

2-Wire Cable   Second
Switch   **3-Wire Cable**   First
Switch

Lamp Off

Switch
Position
Up

Switch
Position
Down

2-Wire
Power
Source
110-120 V

——————— Circuit Completed
— — — — — Circuit Interrupted

Here Is What You Will Need

Materials

- Two three-way switches
- Switch cover plate
- Length of Type NM #14-3 or #12-3 cable with ground (or other cable, as required)
- 2″ x 3″ switch box
- Staples for Type NM cable (or other, as required)
- Electrical tape (optional)
- Length of EMT thinwall (optional)
- EMT thinwall connector (optional)

Tools

- Marking pencil
- Tape measure
- Drill with bits
- Screwdrivers
- Pliers (optional)
- Wire stripper
- Auxiliary light source (optional)
- Hammer
- Stepladder (optional)
- Fish-wire or snake (optional)
- Electrician's diagonal cutters
- Keyhole or saber saw
- Utility knife
- Scratch awl (optional)
- Armored cable cutter (optional)
- Hacksaw (optional)
- Tube bender

thinwall tubing to the box with a thinwall connector — thinwall tubing protects the cable from damage — and then secure both the tubing and the box to the wall or post. If you have access to a tube bender, use it to shape the tubing to lie flat against the surface. In an unfinished area, you can simply staple the Type NM cable to the wood surfaces.

The installation of a new switch box inside a wall is a bit more complicated, but not beyond the capabilities of a do-it-yourselfer. Follow the procedure for installing a new switch box described in "New Lighting Fixtures" earlier in this chapter. With the new switch box in place — either on the surface or built into the wall — run the three-wire cable between the new box and the existing switch box, allowing an extra 6 to 8 inches at both boxes. Clamp the cable in the new box. Strip off the cable cover and remove about ¾ inch of insulation from each of the conductors. Connect the conductors and bare ground wire to the three-way switch according to the accompanying wiring diagram. Attach the cover plate to the new switch box.

Deenergize the circuit to which you are adding the new switch. Then go to the existing on-off switch to attach the new three-way switch and the three-wire cable. Remove the cover plate and the switch-mounting screws, and pull the switch itself out of the box as far as the attached wires allow. Disconnect the wires and remove the on-off switch. Run the three-wire cable into the box and fasten it with a cable clamp. Strip off the cable sheath and remove about ¾ inch of insulation from each of the conductor wires. Connect the line wires and the new-cable conductors and ground wire to the switch according to the accompanying wiring diagram. Mount the switch in the box, attach the cover plate, restore the electric power, and test your new three-way switches.

Installing a Dimmer Switch

Although adding a dimmer switch may seem to be a new installation, the job really is no different than replacing an ordinary on-off switch with another of the same type. In fact, you can change your simple on-off wall switch in a matter of minutes to a dimmer switch that allows you to adjust room light from high brilliance to total darkness. An outgrowth of solid-state electronics, dimmer switches can greatly enhance the lighting effects in your home; but there are some drawbacks to dimmers that you must consider.

The dimmer switch is generally used with incandescent fixtures. Only a few specially built types of fluorescent fixtures can be dimmed, and damage to the dimmer — as well as dismal lighting results — occurs when it is wired to a standard fluorescent fixture. You can, however, obtain dimmers that are designed to be used with certain controllable fluorescent lamp ballasts, at fairly high cost. For best results, limit your dimmer installations to ceiling lamps or chandeliers, and be careful not to exceed the wattage rating for the dimmer you install. If the switch is labeled for 600 watts, for example, use no more than six 100-watt bulbs (or an equivalent amount) in the lighting fixture.

Here Is What You Will Need

Materials

- Dimmer switch
- Solderless connectors (wirenuts)

Tools

- Screwdrivers
- Electrician's diagonal cutters
- Auxiliary light source (optional)
- Wire stripper (optional)
- Razor knife (optional)

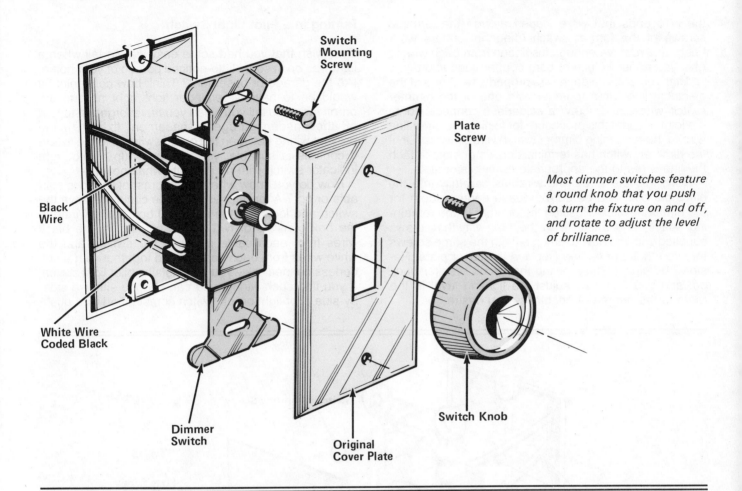

Switch Mounting Screw

Plate Screw

Black Wire

White Wire Coded Black

Dimmer Switch

Original Cover Plate

Switch Knob

Most dimmer switches feature a round knob that you push to turn the fixture on and off, and rotate to adjust the level of brilliance.

Caution: Dimmers are intended solely for lamp adjustment; *never* try to control the operating speed or the heat production of an appliance by using a dimmer.

If the on-off switch that you plan to replace with a dimmer is part of a three-way switch, you must purchase a special kind of dimmer switch; not all dimmers can replace a three-way switch. On the other hand, most dimmer switches are built to fit standard electrical boxes, and you can usually put back the same cover plate that you used for the regular on-off switch. The larger size of the dimmer knob hides the fact that a round shaft protrudes through a rectangular hole.

Most dimmers on the market feature a round knob that you push to turn the fixture on or off, and rotate to adjust for variations in brilliance. There is another version, though, that closely resembles an ordinary on-off switch in appearance. In fact, you can use this type of dimmer as a simple on-off switch. With the switch down all the way, the fixture is off. As you slowly raise the handle, you gradually increase the brilliance until the handle is all the way up and the lamp is as bright as it can be. You should know, however, that a lamp controlled by a dimmer is never as bright as it is when controlled by a traditional on-off switch.

Some kinds of dimmer switches have no terminal screws for the attachment of line wires. Instead, they may have wires that are directly attached to the line wires. Or they may have small holes on the back of the dimmer into which you insert the bare copper ends of the conductors. Locking tabs make the electrical connections, as well as grip the wire so that it cannot pull out. You can, nevertheless, release the wire from the switch by inserting a narrow-bladed screwdriver into the slots next to the wire-grip holes.

Deactivate the circuit containing the on-off switch that you plan to replace with the dimmer switch, and remove the mounting screws from the cover plate. The plate should fall off when you take out the screws, but it may not. Instead, it may be stuck to the wall by several layers of paint. If this is the case, do not attempt to pull the plate free. Use a razor knife to cut through the paint closely around the edge of the plate.

Once the plate is off, remove the two screws that hold the on-off switch in the electrical box. Detach the wires from the terminal screws, and — if it is still in good condition — save the switch for future use. Cut the wire ends that were looped around the terminal screws of the former switch (diagonal cutters work best), and remove enough insulation from each wire to give you about ¾ inch of bare copper conductor.

After you prepare each wire properly, twist one of the electrical line wires together with one of the dimmer switch wires, and screw a solderless connector onto the joint. Repeat this procedure for joining the other line wire to the remaining dimmer switch wire or wires. Or, if the dimmer switch has terminal screws or slots, attach the line wires to the appropriate terminals or slots.

Now, fold the wires and wirenuts carefully into the electrical box, and be sure to leave enough room for the dimmer switch. Position the dimmer in the remaining space, and attach it to the box with the screws supplied with the new dimmer, or with the same screws that you took out earlier. Replace the cover plate. Restore the circuit's fuse or trip the circuit breaker back on, and you can now adjust the lighting level in the room to the degree of brightness you desire.

Putting in a Pilot Light Switch

Ever wish that you had some easy way to tell when a light was on in some little-noticed portion of your home, like the garage or basement? Think how convenient it would be to have a reminder light right next to the on-off switch to tell you when you have forgotten to turn off the unseen garage or basement fixture. If the present wiring between the on-off switch and the fixture it controls is suitable, you can hook up a pilot light indicator switch with no difficulty whatsoever.

How do you know whether the present wiring is suitable or not? After deenergizing the circuit, remove the switch and look into the electrical box; if the wiring in the box consists of two cables coming in, the black wires from each cable going to the switch, and the white wires from each cable joined together with a solderless connector — you can install a pilot light switch. If you find such wiring, you can choose either a side-by-side pilot light/on-off switch combination or a push-

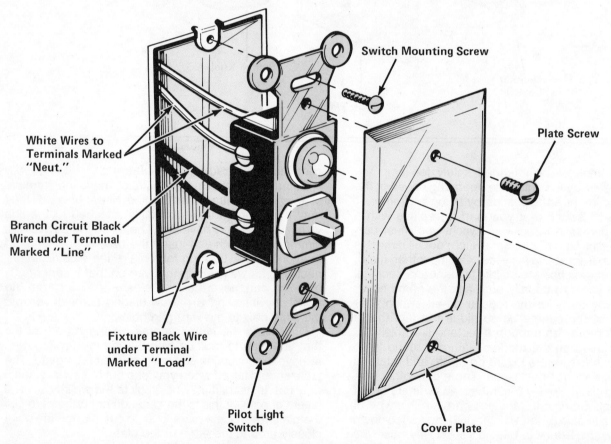

White Wires to Terminals Marked "Neut."

Branch Circuit Black Wire under Terminal Marked "Line"

Fixture Black Wire under Terminal Marked "Load"

Pilot Light Switch

Switch Mounting Screw

Plate Screw

Cover Plate

If an existing switch has two cables coming into the electrical box, with the black wires from each cable going to the switch, and the white wires joined, you can install a pilot light switch. To do so, connect the white wires to the terminals marked "Neut." Connect the branch circuit's black wire to the terminal marked "Line." Finally, connect the fixture's black wire to the terminal marked "Load."

Here Is What You Will Need

Materials

- Combination pilot lamp and push-type switch with lamp in push button (or other type of switch)
- Type 6S6 indicator lamp (or other, as required)
- Receptacle cover plate

Tools

- Screwdrivers
- Electrician's diagonal cutters
- Wire stripper (optional)
- Auxiliary light source (optional)

button switch that contains a small neon glow lamp behind the translucent button. The installation procedures for both types of pilot light switches are nearly identical.

With the circuit dead, disconnect the black wires from the switch. Next take off the solderless connector from the joined pair of white wires, separate them, and fasten them to the pilot light switch under the terminal screws marked "NEUT." If the screws are not marked, attach the white wires under the terminal screws that connect to the screw-in section of the pilot light socket.

Fasten the black wire that comes from the branch circuit under the switch terminal screw marked "LINE," and fasten the black wire that goes to the ceiling light under the terminal screw marked "LOAD." NOTE: If you do not know which is the line wire and which is the ceiling light wire, there is an easy way to find out. Connect the wires and complete the installation; later, when you turn the power back on, you will find that a wrong connection results in the pilot light staying on when the switch is off. To correct the wiring, cut the current once again, disassemble the switch, and interchange the wire connections.

Once you have the pilot light switch wired properly, tuck the wires into the electrical box, push the pilot light switch into place, and fasten the switch to the box with the screws that the manufacturer includes with the switch. Attach the cover plate, screw a bulb into the indicator lamp, and replace the snap-on cover over the pilot light. That completes a rather simple installation, and you now have a pilot light to remind you to turn off the unseen lighting fixture in your home.

Timer Switches

Probably you are already familiar with the portable timing devices that you plug into a receptacle and into which you can plug lamps, appliances and other electrical equipment. You know that one of the most effective home security systems is to have the lights, TV,

and radio go on and off as if someone were at home when no one really is. But do you know that you can install a permanent timer switch in one of your outlets instead of the standard duplex receptacle? Moreover, if you want to hook several receptacles to a timer device, you can install a heavy-duty timer. A heavy-duty timer consists of a circuit run from your home's main entrance panel, through the timer, to as many receptacles as you want to have timer-controlled, provided you do not overload the circuit. People who are often away from their homes should consider installing a heavy-duty timer device to turn television, radio, and lighting fixtures on and off with realistic regularity.

Essentially, the timer is no more than an on-off switch that an electric clock motor trips at preset intervals. It has a dial that is marked for 24 hours, making it easy for you to set the timer for the turn-on hour and the turn-off hour you desire. Most timers are difficult to set right to the minute, but you should be able to set it within about five minutes of the moment you want the circuit on or off; that should be close enough for your purposes.

Installing a Receptacle Timer Switch. Installation of a single permanent timer switch instead of a duplex receptacle is, of course, much easier than putting in a heavy-duty timer. To install the outlet switch, you merely replace the receptacle of your choice with the timer. After you deenergize the appropriate circuit, you can safely remove the cover plate from the receptacle and loosen the receptacle mounting screws. Pull the receptacle out of the electrical box, and disconnect the line wires from the terminal screws. Now, look at the new timer that you plan to install. Does it have a separate mounting plate? If so, attach the mounting plate to the outlet box with the screws provided. You might find, however, that the manufacturer has attached the mounting plate to the timer, just to keep all the parts together. If that is so, detach the plate from the timer and then fasten it to the outlet box as you would if it were packaged separately.

Here Is What You Will Need

Materials

- Receptacle timer switch
- Solderless connectors (wirenuts)

Tools

- Screwdrivers
- Electrician's diagonal cutters
- Auxiliary light source (optional)
- Wire stripper (optional)

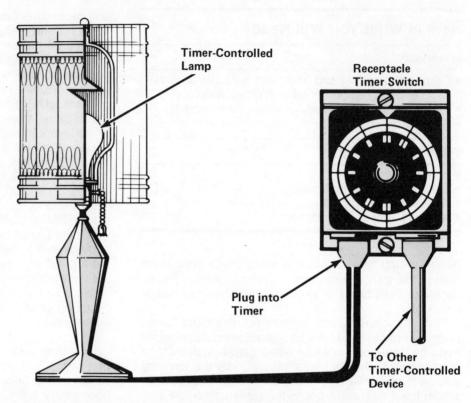

Timer-Controlled Lamp

Receptacle Timer Switch

Plug into Timer

To Other Timer-Controlled Device

To install a receptacle timer switch, you must first deenergize the circuit running to the receptacle that you plan to replace with the timer switch. Then you remove the existing receptacle, install the new timer's mounting plate, connect the outlet wires to the timer according to the manufacturer's instructions, and mount the receptacle timer in place.

Now, attach the timer wires to the circuit wires — using wirenuts, to cover the joints — black wire to black wire, white wire to white wire, and green wire to the ground.

Joining timer wires to circuit wires completes the electrical connections involved in installing a permanent timer switch. Once that is accomplished, all you need do is fasten the timer to its mounting plate, restore power to the circuit, and set the device for the time you want the current on and off. Consult the instructions supplied with your new switch for the details on how to set turn-on and turn-off times.

Installing a Heavy-Duty Timer Switch. Installing a heavy-duty timer is, as mentioned, a bit more complicated. Moreover, you will need to buy a substantial number of electrical materials and supplies. Start with a general-purpose type of timer with a single-pole single-throw (SPST) switch, or a double-pole single-throw (DPST) model for two complete circuits. Before you can complete your shopping list, however, you must prepare a sketch of the new circuit that you plan to control with the timer. For convenience, start by locating the timer near the main entrance panel. Most people who install a heavy-duty timer plan at least two outlets — one in the kitchen and one in the bedroom — to be linked to the timer; but if you have a large home, you may want additional outlets to be governed by the timer. From the sketch, you can determine the length of Type NM cable and the number of octagonal junction boxes, 2-by-3-inch wall boxes, duplex receptacles, and solderless connectors you will need.

Once you have all the materials and supplies required for the installation, you can begin work. Since your last task is connecting the timer-controlled network to the electrical system in your home, you need not deenergize any circuits at the start. You will be working with deenergized circuits throughout the installation until you get into the main panel box at the end.

The first thing to do is to mount the timer box. You may find that the manufacturer packages the timer all assembled; if this is the case, you must remove the screws that hold the timer mechanism in its box to gain access to the mounting holes in the back panel. Take the timer mechanism out of its box and leave it out until later. Mount the timer box in the location that you have selected, using expansion screw anchors or a similar type of fastener if you are attaching the box to a concrete or masonry wall.

Now go to the locations noted in your sketch for the placement of the new receptacles. Follow the procedure outlined in the section "Adding a Receptacle" later in this chapter. However, rather than run the new circuit cable directly to the main panel, route it to the heavy-duty timer.

NOTE: For convenience, segments of the new circuit

Here Is What You Will Need

Materials

- General-purpose timer
- Length of Type NM cable (or other cable, as required)
- 4″ octagonal junction box(es) with blank cover(s)
- 2″ x 3″ receptacle box(es)
- Duplex receptacle(s) with cover plate(s)
- Solderless connectors (wirenuts)
- Cable clamps
- Staples for Type NM cable (or other, as required)
- Timer mounting fasteners
- Miscellaneous hardware
- Electrical tape (optional)

Tools

- Screwdrivers
- Marking pencil
- Tape measure
- Hammer
- Electrician's diagonal cutters
- Auxiliary light source (optional)
- Drill with bits
- Keyhole or saber saw
- Fish-wire or snake (optional)
- Punch (optional)
- Pliers (optional)
- Wire stripper

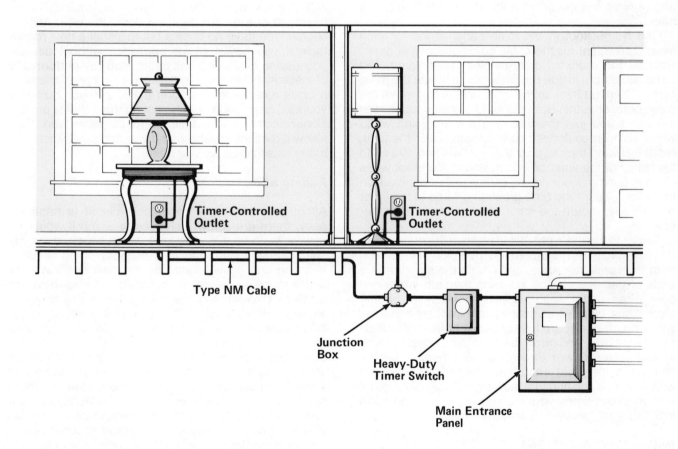

A heavy-duty timer system consists of a circuit run from your home's main entrance panel, through the timer, and to the receptacles that you wish to have timer-controlled.

may be run to and joined at one or more junction boxes before routing the circuit to the heavy-duty timer. To connect two or more cables at a junction box, join black wires to black wires, and white wires to white wires, using wirenuts. Connect one end of a scrap piece of ground wire to the other ground wires with a wirenut. Then, attach the remaining end of the scrap piece of ground wire to the junction box with a ground screw or clip. After the connections have been made, mount the cover on the junction box.

At the timer box near the main entrance panel, remove knockouts from the timer box in the locations most favorable for accommodating the incoming and outgoing cables. Install cable clamps in the timer box knockouts, run the receptacle cable into the timer box, and fasten the clamps.

Caution: Up until now you have not needed to concern yourself about the danger of live circuits, but you have reached the point where you must make the connections to the electrical system. Be careful! Open the door to the main entrance panel, throw the main disconnect to the "off" position — or pull the main fuses — and remove the cover from the main entrance panel box.

Find a knockout in the main panel at the location most convenient for the cable coming from the timer. Remove the knockout disc, install a cable clamp, and run a cable from inside the timer box to inside the main panel. Then, go back to the timer box, and remove the cable outer sheaths. Bare the ends of the conductors in the cable and join the incoming and outgoing white wires, using a solderless connector to cover the joint. Next, following the diagram that you will find affixed to the inside of the timer box door, attach the black wires of the incoming and outgoing cables to the terminals on the timer. Secure the bare grounding wires to the timer box. Finally, mount the timer mechanism in the timer box.

Return to the main panel and remove the outer cover from the cable inside the box. Strip ½ inch of insulation from the conductor ends, and attach the straight bare ends of the wires in the following manner: white and bare wires under separate available screws on the ground bus; black wire under the terminal screw (not the screw head) of a spare fuse or circuit breaker. Replace the panel cover, and throw the main disconnect back on to restore the power throughout your home. Set the timer, and then test each timer-controlled receptacle with a lamp. If you find that the lamp actually does go off and on at the times you set, you know that you have installed your heavy-duty timer properly.

INSTALLING ADDITIONAL RECEPTACLES

How many times have you purchased a new lamp, appliance, home entertainment equipment or other device only to find that there is no electrical outlet near the place that you would like to position the newly acquired item? Undoubtedly, there is at least one room of your home where you need another outlet. Older homes, especially, were not constructed to accommodate all the electrically powered equipment that has come to be considered essential for modern living. Newer homes, wired according to the provisions of the National Electrical Code, must contain no stretch of wall more than 6 feet distant from an electrical outlet. Nevertheless, even newer homes can cause headaches when you find that you do not have an outlet in the exact location you need one.

There are several types of receptacles that you can install, depending on your electrical needs. The simplest way to increase the number of outlets in your home is merely to extend the wiring from an existing outlet to a new receptacle in your chosen location. The primary restriction on such a procedure is that the circuit supplying the present outlet must be able to accommodate the additional load. Sometimes, the problem is that you need an outlet for a specific purpose, like directly behind an electric clock that hangs on a wall. A clock receptacle eliminates the unattractive appearance of the cord dangling down the wall. And, of course, you have no choice but to install a new receptacle if you buy a major appliance without already possessing a 220-240-volt outlet. You can perform any of these installations — extending a receptacle, adding a clock receptacle, installing a 220-240-volt outlet — yourself, saving the substantial charges that a professional electrician would bill you for the same work. Just follow directions carefully, and you can safely install as many receptacles as you need.

Adding a Receptacle

Although extending a receptacle circuit is relatively easy, there are a few instances in which it would be unwise to do so. One instance would be when the circuit is already loaded to near capacity. If the circuit is handling only a light load and the new outlet will not add enough to cause an overload, you will have no problem in extending the wiring; but if the circuit is already heavily loaded, do not use it. Instead, run a totally new circuit from your power distribution panel to the new outlet. Do not extend your wiring to add another receptacle to a bathroom wall, either. For safety's sake, avoid having electrical devices in the bathroom. There is an unpleasant history of plugged-in bathroom appliances that have fallen into occupied tubs with fatal results. Finally, do not extend a kitchen circuit, unless to add a clock or to place a receptacle at some out-of-the-way point for convenience only, and where there is little likelihood that an appliance might be used. Instead, run an entirely new circuit.

On the other hand, suppose that you want to extend a receptacle circuit to some other area, that the existing

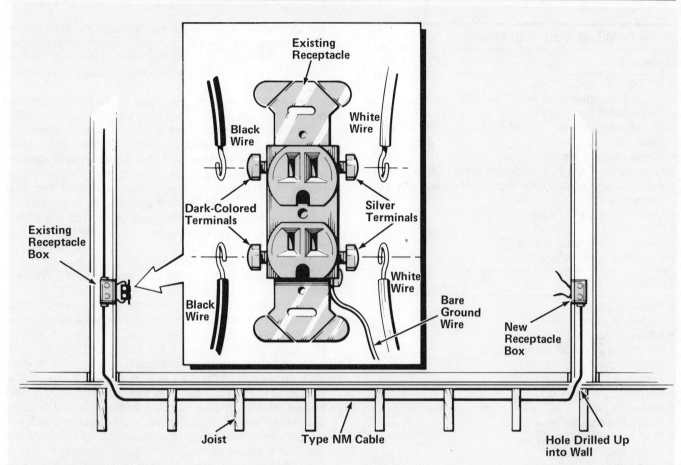

Labels in figure:
- Existing Receptacle
- Black Wire
- White Wire
- Dark-Colored Terminals
- Silver Terminals
- Existing Receptacle Box
- Black Wire
- White Wire
- Bare Ground Wire
- New Receptacle Box
- Joist
- Type NM Cable
- Hole Drilled Up into Wall

If a circuit is able to handle the additional load, you can add a receptacle by extending the wiring from an existing outlet to the new outlet.

circuit can handle an additional load, and that you have access to the space above or below the level of the present and proposed electrical outlets — there is no reason not to go ahead with the project under such conditions.

After you deenergize the circuit, you can start to work on the existing receptacle. Remove the cover plate, loosen the mounting screws, and pull the receptacle out as far as the attached wires permit. Examine the line cable to determine its size; you should use the same size cable for the new outlet. You will probably find it most convenient to use two-conductor nonmetallic sheathed Type NM #12 or #14 gauge cable. If the existing circuit has a bare equipment grounding wire, use Type NM cable with bare ground wire of matching size. If not, either change the entire circuit to a grounded type in the interests of safety and modernization or continue the circuit as an ungrounded one, without the bare conductor, using Type NM wo/g. Under no circumstances should you install a grounding-type three-slot receptacle in an ungrounded circuit — use

the old style two-slot receptacle. If you have access to an uncut length of cable inside the box, you may be able to see the wire size imprinted on the cable's outer sheath. You can, of course, compare the cable with others of known sizes, or measure the diameter of the bare copper conductor with a wire gauge to determine the wire size.

Naturally, there is no way you can figure out how much cable to buy until you decide where you want to locate your new receptacle. You can try to position the new outlet so that the side of the electrical box can be attached to a wall stud, or between studs and secured with plaster clips. The new receptacle should be at a height of about 12 inches up from the floor, but if the other outlets in the room are at a different height, make the new outlet conform to the others for a uniform appearance.

Once you determine precisely where the new receptacle should go, place the electrical outlet box — open end away from you — against the wall and draw a line around it. Do not include any adjustable plaster ears in

Here Is What You Will Need

Materials

- 2″ x 3″ receptacle box
- Duplex receptacle to match existing type
- Receptacle cover plate
- Length of matching Type NM cable (or other cable, as required)
- Cable clamps (optional)
- Staples for Type NM cable (or other, as required)
- Gangable receptacle box, box extension or deep box (as required)
- Miscellaneous hardware
- Plaster clips (optional)
- Scrap copper wire (optional)
- Electrical tape (optional)

Tools

- Marking pencil
- Tape measure
- Screwdrivers
- Electrician's diagonal cutters
- Wire stripper
- Auxiliary light source (optional)
- Stepladder (optional)
- Drill with bits
- Keyhole or saber saw
- Punch (optional)
- Pliers (optional)
- Utility knife
- Fish-wire or snake (optional)
- Wire gauge (optional)
- Scratch awl (optional)
- Armored cable cutter (optional)

your outline. Now, turn the box around so that the open end faces you, and refine your outline to include the corner projections on the box. The finished outline represents the area that you are going to cut out of the wall to accommodate the new receptacle box.

To begin the cutting process, drill ⅝-inch holes at the corners of the outline (the holes should be positioned so that their edges will take care of the projections on the electrical box) through the plaster or drywall and into the hollow part of the wall. Insert a keyhole or saber saw into one of the drilled holes, and cut the wall away carefully along the lines that you drew. When you finish cutting, insert the electrical box in the wall to see whether you cut the hole properly. Refine the hole with the saw, if necessary, to provide a suitable fit for the electrical box, but do not attach the box to the wall yet.

At this point, you need to drill a hole in the floor inside the wall, directly below the outlet hole you just cut. Merely locating the right spot can be a tough job. Try measuring carefully, but if that is unsuccessful, remove the baseboard and drive a nail through the floor down to the basement level to give you a point of reference. Be sure, however, that the spot that you select for the nail will be covered after you put the baseboard back in place.

One way or another, you must find that spot for the hole in the between-wall space, directly below the outlet hole. Once you do, drill a ⅝-inch hole up from the basement level. Feed one end of the new cable through the floor hole, into the between-wall space, and up where you can reach it from the hole you made earlier for the electrical box. You may find that the weight of the cable — combined with the force of gravity — will pull the cable back down into the basement. Work out some way to temporarily support the cable from below, or have a helper hold it, until you can get hold of it. Pull the cable through the hole and hook it over the edge of the outlet hole so that it will not slip back.

Before you can secure the cable in the electrical box, however, you must pry out one of the knockout discs — a screwdriver or punch and pliers does the job well — from one end of the box. If the electrical box you have does not contain internal clamps but does have ½-inch size knockouts, you can use a cable clamp in the knockout to hold the cable in the box. The clamp also serves as a protective bushing to prevent any chafing of the cable as it enters the electrical box. Feed at least 6 inches of cable through the knockout hole and tighten the clamp screw to secure the cable in place.

Push the electrical box — with cable attached — into the wall opening. Fasten the box to the wall stud by driving nails or screws through the holes in the side of the box; or — if you have lath-and-plaster walls — drive screws into the laths through the holes in the adjustable plaster ears. Or install a pair of plaster clips. In any case, make sure that the front edge of the electrical box lines up flush with the surface of the wall.

You can now proceed with the electrical connections at your new outlet. Remove the outer cover from the Type NM cable and strip about ¾ inch insulation from the conductor wires. Attach the conductors to the terminal screws of the new receptacle, and if present, fasten the bare grounding wire first under the grounding terminal and then to the box with a grounding screw or clip. Be sure to loop the conductor wire in a clockwise direction under the heads of the terminal screws. You should also take care to connect the wires so that all the wire without insulation is safely under the screw heads. Clip off any excess uninsulated wire with diagonal cutters. With the wires connected properly, you can fasten the receptacle to the electrical box with the screws provided, and then attach the cover plate to the outlet.

Now, go to the existing outlet and, as you did before, locate a point in the floor inside the wall directly below the outlet. Drill a ⅝-inch hole in the floor from the

Locating the right spot to drill a hole in the floor inside the wall can be a tough job. One way is to remove the baseboard (top, left) and drive a nail through the floor down to the basement level to give you a point of reference. Pry up the shoe molding with a putty knife (top, right), use a screwdriver and a wooden block for leverage (bottom, left) to remove the molding, and use a small pry bar to remove the baseboard (bottom, right).

basement up into the inside wall space; and drill ⅝-inch holes as necessary through the basement joists between the existing outlet and your newly installed receptacle. Your drilled holes should be in a fairly straight path (although they can run at a slight angle), and each one should be at least 2 inches up from the bottom edge of the joist.

Before you can thread the cable through these holes, however, you must do some work on the electrical box at the existing outlet. Remove the box from the wall; remove the screw from the lower cable clamp inside the box; remove the clamp itself; and pry out whichever knockout disc is in the best position to accommodate the new cable. If the 2-by-3-inch box already contains four or more conductors, you must provide a larger one. You can use a so-called "deep box," a box extension or you can gang another box to the original if it is of the gangable type.

Thread the free end of the Type NM cable through the joist holes from the new receptacle to the hole you drilled below the existing outlet. Then comes a tricky assignment; you must feed the cable up through the hole in the floor and pass it through the opening in the wall. If you have trouble, try running a stiff wire through the floor hole up into the wall. Once you get the stiff wire in place, you can pull it out of the opening. Then tape the wire to the end of the Type NM cable down in the basement, and use the wire to help pull the cable up through the opening in the wall.

Once you have enough cable so that you can make the electrical connections, secure it so that it cannot slip back. Go back down to the basement and examine the cable run through the joists. If there are any points where you had to change the direction of the cable run from going through the joists to passing alongside a joist, make sure that you did not put any sharp right-angle bends in the cable that could weaken the copper conductors and damage the insulation. The way to change direction in a run is to put a generous loop in the cable. If you do run cable alongside a joist, fasten a staple not more than 12 inches from the hole where the cable emerges, and then at least every 4½ feet along the run.

With the cable linked to both the new outlet box and the existing receptacle location, go to the existing receptacle and prepare the new Type NM cable for its electrical connections. Slip the cable into the box, along with the existing cables if you had to remove them to get the box out, tighten the cable clamps and slip the box back into the wall. Remove the outer cable cover; bare the wire ends; and attach white wire to silver terminal, black wire to dark-colored terminal. If they are present, pigtail the new and existing cables' ground wires to the receptacle grounding screw and to the box with a grounding clip or screw. Reconnect the other line wires to their proper terminals.

Caution: Make all connections under terminal screws, but never try to attach two conductors under the same screw head — it is considered an unsafe electrical procedure. You will find two screws on each side of the receptacle; they are provided just for what you are doing; extending wiring without making any splices. If you have three black wires and three white wires, connect one of each to appropriate receptacle terminal screws. Join, or "pigtail," each of the two remaining pairs with wirenuts to short lengths of scrap wire, and connect the pigtail ends of the scrap wire to the appropriate receptacle terminal screws that remain. Pigtail ground wires to the receptacle grounding screw and to the box.

When you finish attaching wires to the terminal screws, put the existing receptacle back into its box and fasten it down with the same screws that you removed earlier. Attach the cover plate, restore the circuit's fuse or trip the circuit breaker, and test your new receptacle with a table lamp.

Wiring a Clock Receptacle

Since the standard location for electrical outlets is about 12 inches up from floor level, many people are dismayed when they hang a new wall clock and see the cord stretching all the way down the wall to the receptacle. Of course, you can eliminate such an unattractive sight by limiting the clocks in your home to those that sit on a table, or by using battery-powered wall clocks, but there is probably at least one place in your home where a 110-120-volt wall-hung clock would be just right. What can you do?

The ideal solution is to put an electrical box in the wall immediately behind the spot where you want the clock to go. Then, you can install a clock receptacle in the box, and hang the clock over the outlet to hide the entire electrical connection. Since the clock outlet has a recessed receptacle that is deep enough to hold the entire plug, the end result is an electric clock that operates with no visible cord whatsoever.

There are several ways to wire a clock receptacle. If there is a circuit with an existing outlet nearby, you can extend the wiring to the new clock receptacle. Follow the instructions described earlier for "Adding a Receptacle," and run the Type NM wiring from the existing receptacle into the attic (or basement), through the joists, and out into the wall behind the clock outlet. If there is no existing circuit nearby, you can hook the new clock receptacle directly to your home's main electrical panel by following the same procedures outlined for installing "New Lighting Fixtures." There is yet another way to wire a clock receptacle, a procedure that is most effective when there is a receptacle in the next room on the other side of the wall. In such a case, you can run the wiring up from that other receptacle. Since an electric clock motor consumes very little electrical power — typically 2 to 5 watts — the clock outlet adds

Here Is What You Will Need

Materials

- 2″ x 3″ switch box (2½″ deep)
- Cable clamps
- Clock receptacle
- Length of Type NM #14-2 or #12-2 cable with ground wire if necessary (or other cable, as required)
- Solderless connectors (optional)
- Plaster clips (optional)
- Miscellaneous hardware
- Electrical tape (optional)

Tools

- Marking pencil
- Tape measure
- Screwdrivers
- Electrician's diagonal cutters
- Auxiliary light source (optional)
- Stepladder (optional)
- Keyhole or saber saw
- Drill with bits
- Wire stripper
- Scratch awl (optional)
- Fish-wire or snake (optional)
- Armored cable cutter (optional)

practically nothing to a branch circuit load.

Measure the distance from the new clock outlet to the existing receptacle, and use this information to obtain the correct length of Type NM cable. If you plan to do a great deal of electrical wiring in your home, you should compare the per-foot cost of a specific length of Type NM cable with the price of a 50-, 100-, or 250-foot coil of cable; purchasing cable by the box may be more economical for you.

Your selection of the location for the new clock outlet will, of course, depend on where you think the clock looks best in the room, but there are some practical considerations involved. The electrical box can be affixed to a wall stud or between studs (studs in the walls are usually 16 inches apart), but you should position it between the same two studs that run on either side of the existing receptacle on the other wall. Hold the electrical box up in the location you choose, outline it, and cut the hole in the wall, as described in "Adding a Receptacle" — but do not mount it yet.

Go to the existing outlet on the other side of the wall and, with the circuit deenergized, remove the cover plate, loosen the receptacle mounting screws, and pull the receptacle out as far as the attached wires allow. If the box is readily removable, take it out too for easier cable-pulling. Loosen the cable clamp in the box, and remove the knockout disc that is in the most convenient spot for running a cable to the clock outlet. Feed the

Type NM cable from the existing box to the hole you cut earlier for the new electrical box. (On the other hand, you may find it handier to feed the cable in the opposite direction — from the hole in the wall to the existing box.) In any case, clamp the new cable to the box. Remove the cable sheath and about ¾ inch insulation from the conductors. Attach the conductors to the spare terminal screws on the existing receptacle, and the ground wire — if present — first to the receptacle terminal and then to the box with a grounding clip. Loop the conductor wires in a clockwise direction under the screw heads; clip off any excess uninsulated wire with diagonal cutters. If there are already two cables connected to the receptacle (all the mounting screws are occupied), you must use short scrap wire lengths and solderless connectors to parallel the cables (that is, pigtail them) to attach them to the receptacle. **Caution:** Never place more than one wire under each screw. After you finish all the wiring connections at the existing outlet, replace the box, receptacle, and cover plate.

At the clock outlet hole, run the other end of the cable through a knockout opening in the new electrical box, and fasten it in position with the cable clamp. Place the box in the wall opening, and attach it securely. After you mount the electrical box, strip off the outer cover from the cable inside the box, bare the wire ends, attach them to the clock receptacle, and fasten the bare wire for grounding to the box with a grounding screw or clip. Install the clock receptacle itself in the box by merely inserting and tightening the two screws that come with the clock outlet.

That nearly completes the job. All you have to do is restore the power by replacing the fuse or flipping the circuit breaker on, and then hang the clock. Of course, you are going to have to do something about that long length of cord that was meant to drape unattractively down your wall. Before you start chopping out a segment of the cord, however, examine the backside of your clock. Some clocks contain a recessed area in which you can coil up the excess cord before you insert the plug into the outlet.

If your clock does not have such a space, then you can shorten the cord. Determine how much cord you need so that you can insert the plug while holding the clock close to its wall mount. Add 3 inches to that length so that you will be able to lift the clock to set the time without disconnecting the plug from the outlet. Cut the cord, attach a new plug, set the time, and hang the clock.

Installing a 220-240-Volt Receptacle

If you own a new home — or an older home that has been rewired — you can plug in major appliances without a second thought. If, on the other hand, your home has never been wired for 220-240-volt current, you cannot install many of the current-consuming equipment

Here Is What You Will Need

Materials

- 220-240-volt receptacle assembly
- Length of ¾" or 1" EMT thinwall (if necessary)
- EMT clamps (optional)
- Length of Type NM cable (or other cable)
- ¾" or 1" setscrew thinwall fitting (if necessary)
- Staples for Type NM cable (or other, as required)
- Double-pole circuit breaker (if necessary)
- Miscellaneous hardware
- Electrical tape (optional)

Tools

- Marking pencil
- Tape measure
- Screwdrivers
- Electrician's diagonal cutters
- Wire stripper
- Hammer
- Auxiliary light source (optional)
- Stepladder (optional)
- Adjustable wrench (optional)
- Drill with bits
- Hacksaw or tubing cutter
- File
- Reamer
- Scratch awl (optional)
- Fish-wire or snake (optional)
- Utility knife
- Pliers (optional)

that modern homemakers have come to depend on. For example, you buy a new electric dryer or range or window air conditioner, and when it arrives you are told: "You can't plug it into a 110-120-volt outlet; you need 220-240 for it." What can you do then? Install a 220-240-volt receptacle yourself!

The first thing to do is examine the plug on the end of the appliance cord. The configuration of blades and prongs is your guide to purchasing the correct receptacle; the receptacle must have holes that match the plug's projections. Buying the correct receptacle is not always an easy task, however. There are many varieties, and some are similar in appearance. To be safe, make a sketch of the plug, and take the sketch with you when you shop for a new receptacle.

Now you need to draw another sketch, showing the proposed wiring installation from the main entrance panel to the location of the new outlet; for illustration, we will choose a basement clothes dryer installation. Make some careful measurements and calculate the length of cable that you will need to connect the 220-240-volt receptacle to your home's electrical system. Be sure to allow for the extra 6 to 8 inches of cable length you will need to go into the receptacle box as well as into the main entrance panel. Buy the type of cable recommended by your supplier, or specified by local electrical code, for the particular job at hand. While the type may not be Type NM, it will handle in much the same way.

In addition to the cable, you may need a length of thinwall tubing to protect that portion of the cable that runs from the outlet up to the ceiling, unless the cable will be concealed within the wall. The term "thinwall" is actually trade jargon for what is properly called electri-

When installing a 220-240-volt receptacle, be sure to obtain the proper receptacle. There are many types for different purposes, and some of them are similar in appearance.

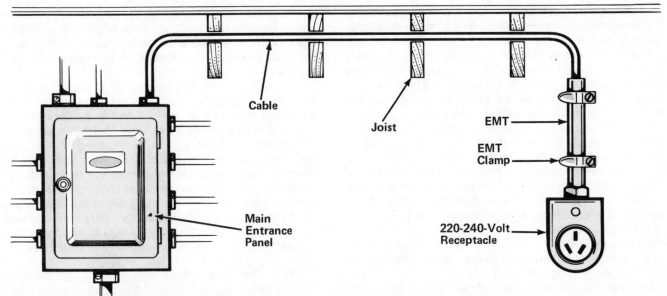

A length of electrical metallic tubing (EMT), or "thinwall," may be needed to protect the portion of the cable leading from the ceiling to the receptacle, unless the cable will be concealed within the wall.

cal metallic tubing (EMT). EMT is a steel tube, somewhat thinner than the steel pipes you see in your home's plumbing system, and is designed for electrical installations. You can buy EMT in 10-foot sections, and then cut it to the lengths required for your specific needs. You can use a tubing cutter for the job, but a hacksaw works well too if you are careful. Ream the cut end of the tubing to remove any sharp burrs or edges; remember, the entire idea behind installing thinwall tubing is to prevent anything from scraping or damaging the cable.

To attach the length of EMT to the receptacle box, you will need a thinwall fitting. You can choose from three types: one requires an indenter tool that impresses a ring of dimples on the fitting after you position the fitting on the tubing; the second type compresses the fitting on the tubing when you tighten a nut; and the third secures to the EMT with a setscrew. Since the latter requires no special tools, this fitting is probably the best one for the do-it-yourselfer. When installing a 220-240-volt receptacle, you complete nearly the entire set of procedures before you hook the new outlet into your home's electrical system. Therefore, you need not deenergize any circuits until you are well into your work. Once you know where you want the new receptacle to be located (convenient connections to your appliances should be your primary consideration) and have the required materials, you can begin to install your new 220-240-volt receptacle.

Measure the distance from the ceiling down to the top of the receptacle, and cut your thinwall tubing to that length. Once you are sure that the cut end is totally

free of sharp projections and that the inner rim is smooth, connect the thinwall tubing to the receptacle box using a thinwall fitting. Fasten the thinwall tubing to the wall with EMT clamps. Also fasten the receptacle box to the wall. Use wood screws if the box and tubing are to be mounted on a wooden wall and expansion anchors if they are to be affixed to a concrete or masonry wall. Install EMT clamps at the top, at the bottom, and at 3-foot intervals between the top and bottom of the thinwall tubing.

Feed the cable down from the top of the thinwall, through the tubing (or through wall, ceiling or floor cavities as necessary), and into the outlet box. Once the cable is in position, secure it with a staple at the point where it enters the thinwall at the top. Since the fitting that holds the thinwall tubing to the receptacle box possesses no means for gripping the cable, the staple at the top is the only way to hold the cable in place. Next, bare the wire ends in the outlet box and attach the wires under the receptacle's terminal screws. You should find printed indications adjacent to the screws instructing you as to which wire — red, black, white and ground (bare or green) — goes to each screw. Place the cover on the box. That completes the wiring connections at the receptacle box; now you can begin the procedures for linking the receptacle to your home's electrical system.

Caution: The first procedure, of course, is to deenergize the main entrance panel. Open the panel door and turn off the main disconnect to cut the current throughout your home. The second procedure is to bring the cable from the point where it leaves the thinwall tubing, through holes drilled in joists, by stapling to framing members or maneuvering it through structural cavities, to the main panel.

Remove the outer cover from the main entrance panel box. Find a knockout in the main panel box at the location most convenient to the circuit to which the new cable will be connected. Remove the knockout disc and use a cable clamp to fasten the cable to the box. Remove the outer cover from the cable inside the main entrance box. Strip ½ inch insulation from the conductor ends, and attach the straight, bare ends of the wires in the following manner: white and ground (bare or green) wires under separate unoccupied screws on the ground bus; red and black wires under the two terminal screws of a double-pole circuit breaker. Either use a spare 220-240-volt circuit breaker or install a new double-pole unit, which is installed in the same way as a single-pole circuit breaker, as described in the following section "Adding a Branch Circuit."

Replace the cover on the main panel and throw the main disconnect to "on." That completes the installation, and you now have a 220-240-volt receptacle ready to supply power to your new appliance.

ADDING A BRANCH CIRCUIT

Did it ever occur to you as you thought about installing a new lighting fixture, standard duplex receptacle or 220-240-volt receptacle that there might not be the required spare branch circuit breaker in your home's main entrance panel? What can you do if all the existing circuits are loaded close to their capacity? Are you forever limited to the number of circuits that you have in your home at present? Fortunately, in many instances you can add the new branch circuits that you need to complete various fixture and receptacle installations.

There are, of course, many types of electrical main entrance panels. The principles involved in adding a new circuit are, however, fairly standard for all makes and models. The procedures are essentially the same, and the parts are quite similar. If you see unoccupied prepunched spaces on the front cover of your main panel, you can probably add new circuits to the electrical system. Those spaces on the panel are provided for knockout removal and the addition of branch circuits. NOTE: In a few instances, that may be no actual circuit provisions built in behind the knockout blanks, where the cover is a "universal" type that fits several sizes of entrance panels.

Like any electrical work, adding a new branch circuit requires some advance planning. Determine how many lights, appliances, and so forth you want to place on the new circuit. Then add up the total wattage that would be consumed were you to use all the devices simultaneously. The total wattage required tells you what size wire you must install. Assume, for example, that the total load on the new circuit will not exceed

1,440 watts; that means you can install a 15-ampere circuit breaker and 14-2 w/g Type NM cable. Inside the door of the main entrance panel you will find a label; the label provides the information you need to buy the right size and type of circuit breaker.

The new circuitry and new lighting fixtures, switches or duplex receptacles are installed by using the same basic procedures that are outlined in earlier sections, as in "New Lighting Fixtures" and "Installing Additional Receptacles." After you have installed the fixtures, switches and receptacles of the new circuit, you are ready to add the circuit breaker to the main entrance panel; but you must devote a good deal of thought as to how you are going to do this part of the job without endangering your safety. **Caution:** Any time you work inside the main entrance panel you face an electrical hazard. You must, therefore, make this your chief concern.

NOTE: For convenience, segments of the new circuit may be run to and joined at one or more junction boxes before routing the circuit to the main entrance panel. To connect two or more cables at a junction box, join black

Here Is What You Will Need

Materials

- 15- or 20-ampere circuit breaker(s) to fit main entrance panel
- Cable clamp(s)
- Length of Type NM cable (or other cable, as required)
- Staples for Type NM cable (or other, as required)
- Electrical box(es)
- Wall switch(es)
- Duplex receptacle(s)
- Miscellaneous hardware
- Lighting fixture(s)
- Electrical tape (optional)

Tools

- Marking pencil
- Tape measure
- Hammer
- Punch (optional)
- Screwdrivers
- Electrician's diagonal cutters
- Wire stripper
- Drill with bits
- Pliers (optional)
- Auxiliary light source (optional)
- Utility knife
- Stepladder (optional)
- Fish-wire or snake (optional)
- Keyhole or saber saw
- Armored cable cutter (optional)

wires to black wires, and white wires to white wires, using wirenuts. Connect one end of a scrap piece of ground wire to the other ground wires with a wirenut. Then attach the remaining end of the scrap piece of ground wire to the junction box with a ground screw or clip. After the connections have been made, mount the cover on the junction box.

Since the main panel is often located in a place where you (standing in a position to work on it) could possibly be grounded, you would be smart to place a sheet of dry plywood on the floor and to remain *on* the plywood while you add a new circuit breaker in the panel. Most importantly, learn about the main panel; if you know what you are doing, then you can work safely inside the box.

Throw the main breaker to cut off the flow of current throughout your home. The wires that go into the panel from the meter are connected to busses (you can usually identify the busses as the metal pieces that look like tarnished silver), and the busses carry current to the circuit breakers. **Caution:** These wires and the top connecting lugs are still energized; *never touch them!* It is possible, in fact, to install a new circuit breaker without contacting anything other than the plastic circuit breaker housing. Work with care; you must avoid touching an energized area. You may be able to wedge or tape a piece of corrugated cardboard — a good insulator — across the top of the panel box for extra protection.

Remove the front cover from the main panel, and lay it aside. Inspect the panel and make sure that you know which parts are "hot" and must not be touched under any circumstances. Now, inspect your new circuit breaker; you will see that one end is shaped to latch onto a metal tab inside the main panel box, and that the other end is a copper (or silver) conductor clip that hooks into the bus bar. Before you attempt to install the circuit breaker, be certain that you understand just how it snaps into place. You must be able to visualize exactly how it is supposed to go in before you actually try to insert the new circuit breaker.

Hold the circuit breaker at its outer position near the switch handle. It takes only a moment to latch it under the support tab and to snap the conductor clip into the bus bar. Fasten the new circuit breaker into position, and make sure that it is secure and in the "off" position before you go on to the following procedures.

Remove a panel knockout so that the circuit breaker handle can protrude through the opening. That completes the circuit breaker part of the installation; now you are ready to run the cable for the new branch circuit to the new circuit breaker. Remove a knockout from the top, side or bottom of the main panel, depending on which one is most conveniently positioned to accommodate the new cable. Install a cable clamp in the knockout hole, run the cable into the main panel, leaving a suitably long length with which to make con-

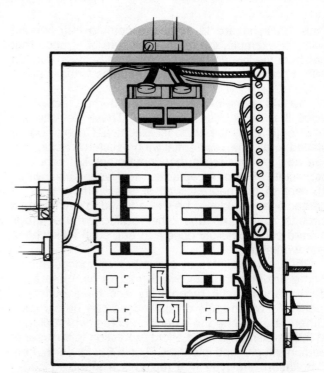

Although you have cut off power by throwing the main breaker, the wires coming into the main entrance panel from the electric meter and the wires' connecting lugs in the panel are still energized! You must not touch them. For protection, tape a piece of corrugated cardboard over this area.

nections and then arrange the conductors along the outside walls of the panel, out of the way; then tighten the clamp on the cable.

Strip the outer sheath from the cable inside the box, and bare each conductor end for a distance of about ½ inch. Loosen the terminal screw on the new circuit breaker, slide the straight black wire end under the terminal screw (not the screw head) and tighten the screw. Fasten the white and bare wires in the same way under separate unoccupied screws on the ground bus. That completes all of the main panel electrical connections; put the cover back on. Throw the main breaker and the new circuit breaker to their energized positions, and you can enjoy the convenience of an additional branch circuit in your home.

ADDING A GROUND FAULT INTERRUPTER

GFI is electricians' shorthand for a new device called the ground fault interrupter (sometimes also called a GFCI, or ground fault circuit interrupter). This is a protective device that not only trips out when an overload or a short circuit occurs, but also senses any leakage of current from a "hot" line to ground. Only a tiny faction of an ampere of current leakage is enough to trip the device and open the circuit. Reaction time is so fast that shock hazard to someone coming into contact with, for example, the metal enclosure of a range that has become live and at the same time being in contact with a good ground, like a waterpipe, is virtually eliminated.

The GFI is one of the best safety and protective devices that have been developed. These devices are now required by the National Electrical Code to be installed in all new residential wiring systems as protective devices on circuits that contain any bathroom receptacles, outdoor receptacles, and receptacles within 15 feet of the nearest wall of a swimming pool. A homeowner would also be well advised to use them on circuits running to any other outlets where shock hazard could possibly pose a threat, such as kitchens and workshops.

GFI's are available in a number of configurations. Some are plug-in units, which merely plug into standard branch circuit receptacles and have outlets in them into which tools or appliances can be plugged. Others are attached to extension cords, which plug in in the usual manner and afford protection to the user of equipment plugged into the GFI unit. But for permanent installation, the type that replaces a standard circuit breaker in a main entrance panel or load center is the best bet. Any circuit that contains outlets for bathroom, outdoor, kitchen, workshop or any other potentially hazardous receptacles can be protected with a GFI by simply removing the original circuit breaker and replacing it with a GFI of appropriate rating. The GFI must, of

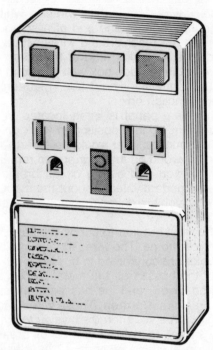

Ground fault interrupters (GFIs) are available in a number of configurations. Some, such as the one illustrated, are plug-in units.

Here Is What You Will Need

Materials

- GFI circuit breaker
- Circuit breaker subpanel (optional)
- Length of Type NM cable (or other cable, as required — optional)
- Type NM cable clamps (or other, as required — optional)
- Type NM cable staples (or other, as required — optional)
- Miscellaneous hardware

Tools

- Screwdrivers
- Electrician's diagonal cutters (optional)
- Wire stripper (optional)
- Hammer (optional)
- Scratch awl (optional)
- Tape measure (optional)
- Utility knife (optional)
- Armored cable cutter (optional)
- Auxiliary light source (optional)

course, be designed to fit the particular brand of main entrance panel in question; making the change is easily done by following the procedures outlined earlier in the section "Adding a Branch Circuit." Naturally, a new circuit can be ground-fault protected in the same way by installing a GFI instead of a conventional circuit breaker.

If no GFI-type circuit breaker is available to fit your particular brand and style of main entrance panel, or if your house is equipped with a fuse-type panel, you can still add GFI protection. Purchase a GFI breaker and a small subpanel into which it will fit. Mount the subpanel close to the main entrance panel. Remove the cable of the circuit that you want to protect from the main entrance panel and route it into the new subpanel, and attach the black "hot" wire to the GFI and the neutral and bare ground wires to separate screws on the ground bus. (NOTE: For a GFI to be effective, the existing circuit must already have a ground wire. If it does not, you may have a professional electrician do the work necessary to add grounded circuitry.) Then run a new length of cable from the subpanel input connecting terminals or lugs back into the main entrance panel and connect the conductors and ground wire in place of the original ones. The ampere rating of the new GFI breaker and the existing fuse or circuit breaker should be the same, and both should match the ampacity of the circuit conductors.

Special Wiring Installations

If you think that electrical repairs and replacements — or new installations of lamps, switches, and circuits — represent the limit of what you can do with the electrical system in your home, then you are in for a pleasant surprise. Do you know, for example, that you can enjoy the protection of an intrusion and fire alarm system without spending a small fortune for a professional installation? If not, keep reading — because all you have to do is purchase a relatively inexpensive kit and follow the instructions outlined in this chapter.

The same is true for other special wiring situations, including home intercoms and garage door openers. You can even wire your entire home to carry the sound of your stereo system to rooms far from the system itself. Finally, you can tackle the electrical wiring requirements of built-in appliances — the garbage disposer, dishwasher, and electric range. Put it all together and you will discover that many of the electrical installations that can make your home a more distinctive, attractive, and convenient place in which to live are well within the grasp of the informed do-it-yourselfer.

INSTALLING A HOME SECURITY SYSTEM

Although there are many kinds of home security systems on the market, homeowners seem to like one particular kind over all the rest. This is the one that turns on a loud bell whenever an intruder breaks open a door or a window. Quite similar to burglar alarms used in stores and offices, this system is sold in kit form, and can be purchased at many hardware stores. You should find the system easy to install, and there can be little doubt that you will be pleased with the protection it affords.

Installation involves mounting the bell in a location where it can be easily heard, attaching a circuit of magnet-operated switches to the bell, and connecting a battery to the system. Since the bell operates from the battery, it remains an effective alarm system even in the event of a power failure.

In electrical terminology, this alarm system is called a closed-circuit system. When the doors and windows are shut, the attached switches are closed. Because all the switches are in a wiring loop, opening any one of them breaks the loop and triggers the bell-ringing circuit. Simply reclosing the door or window, moreover, does not restore the switch loop circuit continuity and does not stop the bell from ringing. The bell continues to ring until either the battery becomes exhausted or

Here Is What You Will Need

Materials

Alarm kit or individual components:
- Bell with built-in solid-state switch
- Magnet switches
- Loop wire
- Batteries
- Bell wire
- Key switch
- Solderless connectors
- Mounting hardware
- Fire sensor switches (optional)
- Window foil tape and terminals (optional)
- Bell enclosure (optional)
- Tamper switch (optional)

Tools

- Drill with bits
- Hammer
- Screwdrivers
- Electrician's diagonal cutters
- Stepladder (optional)
- Auxiliary light source (optional)
- Wire stripper
- Utility knife
- Marking pencil
- Scratch awl
- Tape measure

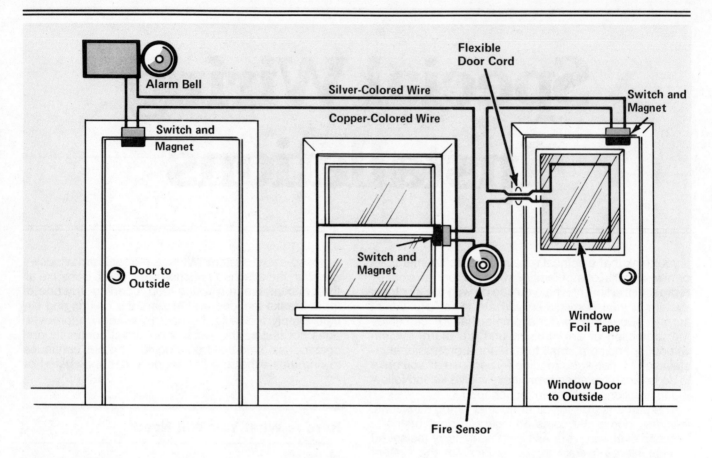

Because all switches in this closed-circuit system are in a wiring loop, opening any one of them breaks the loop and triggers the bell-ringing circuit.

someone switches off the circuit from battery to bell.

Built into the bell is an electronic switch that is turned on by breaking the magnet-switch loop. A key-operated switch in the battery-and-bell circuit allows you to turn the alarm system completely off when it is not needed, and once the alarm goes on, operating the key switch is the only way to silence the bell. Moreover, only someone who has a key to the switch can reset the system.

The magnet-operated switch device consists of two parts that look much alike: one small plastic box contains a strong magnet; the other contains the actual switch. When magnet and switch are not near each other, the switch contacts are separated and the switch is open. On the other hand, when the magnet and switch are near each other, the switch contacts move together and the switch closes. The magnet part of the device is screwed to a door or window, and the switch part is screwed to the door or window frame. Thus, opening a door or window separates magnet from switch, causing the switch to open and trigger the alarm.

The three electronic parts comprising the solid-state switch of the alarm bell are mounted on a circuit board.

Under the circuit board are a solenoid coil and the plunger that strikes the bell. Below the coil is a set of breaker points that causes the plunger to vibrate up and down, which, of course, makes the bell ring. If the system did not include the breaker points, the bell would merely provide a single gong when operated from the direct current of a battery.

Begin the installation with the bell. Decide where you want it located, either to attract the most attention for help or to scare away an intruder. If you decide to mount the bell outdoors, you must drill a hole through the wall for the wires. To shield the bell from the weather, you should install it in a protective metal box of the type made especially for alarm bells. Inside the box is a bracket for mounting a tamper switch—one that sets off the alarm system if someone tries to open the bell box. Located in the side of the box is the key switch—an electric switch built like a lock and operated by a key — that allows a person having a key (but none other) to activate, service, reset or deactivate the alarm system.

If you want the bell to be located indoors, you need not install it in a protective metal box. Mount the bell on the wall in a place where it can be heard easily. Locating an indoor bell in a closet or other confined space is not recommended.

In the kit you should find a mounting backplate attached to the bell by a mounting screw. Remove the nut, and separate the backplate from the bell. You will see a pattern of holes in the backplate. Using wood screws, toggle bolts or other suitable fasteners, attach the backplate to the wall at the place you have chosen to position the bell. Mount the backplate with enough fasteners to hold the bell solidly in place. Be sure that the backplate is mounted right side up, and that the correct side is forward. Usually, there is a tongue on the backplate that should be at the top when the backplate is mounted properly. Do not connect the bell to the backplate until later, however.

You will find that the protective box for an outdoor installation already contains a built-in backplate. Mount the box in the desired location.

Next, install the door and window switches. The magnet part goes on the door or window, while the switch part goes on the window frame or door jamb. Use the mounting screws in the kit to attach the parts. Try to position the two parts of the switch so that they are quite close together—almost touching—when the window or door is closed, and widely separated when the door or window just starts to open.

If you wish, you can include fire sensor switches in the loop of entry-detection switches. Use the kind of fire sensor switch that breaks the loop when the air temperature in its vicinity reaches 135° Fahrenheit. Since that is more than the air temperature is ever likely to reach normally — except in attics, furnace rooms or over wood or coal stoves, or other high-heat producers — you will never experience false alarms during hot weather. Install 190°F sensors in normally hot locations. You should mount the fire sensor switches in the spots where you feel they will be most effective, and there is no reason that you cannot put one or more in every room that you wire for the security system.

Consider using current-conducting window foil tape for additional security. Silver foil with a self-adhesive backing is probably available where you purchase your alarm system, and it is designed to trigger the alarm if an intruder breaks the glass in a door or a window. During installation, make sure there are no breaks in the foil that you stick on the glass; the tape must be continuous. Self-adhesive foil terminals or connectors at the ends of the foil tapes allow you to connect the loop circuit wiring, and a flexible door cord allows you to open a foil-taped door or window without setting off the alarm system.

After you have mounted the bell backplate and installed all the switches, fire sensors, and window foil, it is time to wire the system together. The wire for the entry-detection switch loop is a thin (nearly transparent) two-wire cord that is quite inconspicuous when you

run up the corner of a wall, down a door frame or alongside the baseboard. Use your own good judgment as to what route the wiring should take to attract the least attention.

Start at the point farthest away from the bell (the foil taped to a window or door glass, for example). Using a knife or wire stripper, bare about ¾ inch of the wire ends. Loop each wire end under a separate terminal screw on the switch or door cord. Without cutting the two-wire cord, route it to the next device — a magnet switch, for example. Use small staples to keep the wire runs neat, but be careful not to damage the wire when you hammer in the staples. At the second device, use a knife to split apart the side-by-side conductors for a distance of a few inches. Cut apart just one of the wires — the copper-colored wire — not both! Bare about ¾ inch of the copper wire ends and connect them to the switch's terminal screws.

Continue in this manner to the next switch, cutting apart only the copper-colored wire in the cord and attaching the bared ends of the cut wire under the terminal screws on the switch. One after the other, run the wire to all the entry-detection switches and fire sensors, finally running the two-wire cord to the bell backplate location.

If you need more than the spool of wire (usually 100 feet) that is included in security system kits, obtain another spool, and start the new length at the last switch reached by the first length of wire. Cut off what remains of the first length of wire at the switch, and bare the two conductors in both wires. Attach the copper-colored wires to the switch terminal screws. Twist together the two silver-colored wires, and affix a small solderless connector to them. Then, continue the run back to the bell with the new spool of wire, but do not connect the wire to the bell yet.

You have just finished wiring the intruder-entry sensor switch loop. If you did it properly, the circuit of the copper-colored wire will go to and *through* all the switches, and the silver-colored wire will return from the farthest end with *no* breaks or interruptions.

Now it is time to install the battery circuit. Obtain two 6-volt lantern-type batteries, or a suitable type of rechargeable battery pack — wet or dry. Decide where you are going to locate the batteries; they can be hidden in a closet, a cabinet or placed on a shelf you can install for that purpose. The kit should contain some ordinary bell wire — lengths of single-conductor wire. One should be covered with red insulation and the other black. Use this wire for connecting the batteries to the bell.

In the battery-to-bell circuit, you must connect the positive (+) and negative (−) terminals of the battery to the bell to make the solid-state switches operate properly. Notice that the bell wire ends also are black and red. Such color coding helps you to wire the battery to the bell correctly. Run both a black and a red wire from

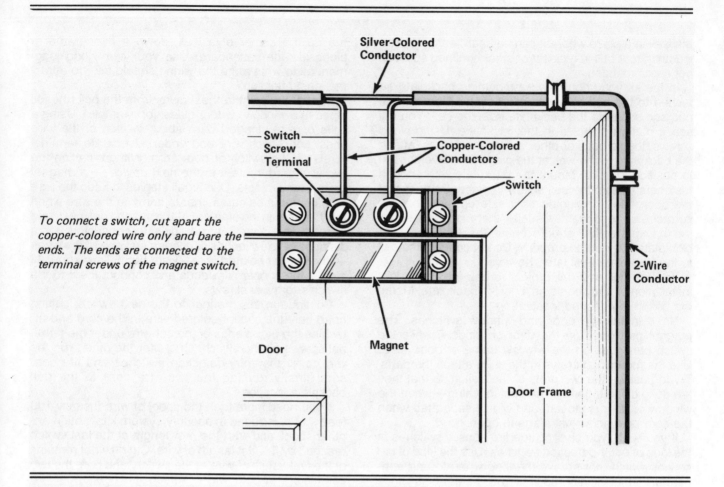

Silver-Colored
Conductor

Switch
Screw
Terminal

Copper-Colored
Conductors

Switch

To connect a switch, cut apart the
copper-colored wire only and bare the
ends. The ends are connected to the
terminal screws of the magnet switch.

2-Wire
Conductor

Door

Magnet

Door Frame

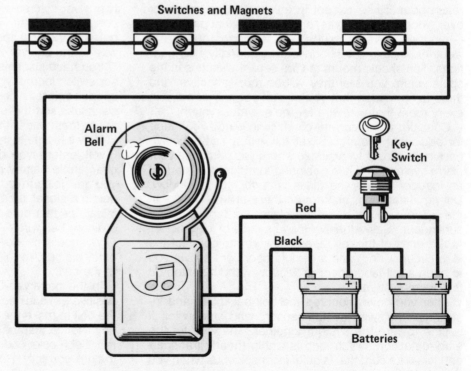

Switches and Magnets

Alarm
Bell

Key
Switch

The diagram shows how the closed-
circuit wiring loop is connected to
a key switch, the alarm bell, and
the batteries.

Red

Black

Batteries

the bell location to the battery location. Connect the red wire to the positive (+) terminal of one of the cells, and connect the black wire to the negative (−) terminal of the other cell. Later on, as a last step, you will connect a wire between the negative (−) terminal of the first cell and the positive (+) terminal of the other cell. While you are working on the installation, you just might accidentally touch the black and red wires together. Since that would quickly discharge the batteries, you should leave the between-the-cells section of wire out until last.

Now it is time to connect the bell. Use solderless connectors to join the black wire from the battery to the black wire of the bell, and the red wire from the battery to the red wire of the bell. If your installation includes a key switch, however, run the red wire first to the key switch and then to the bell. At the key switch, cut the red wire, strip insulation from the ends, and fasten each cut end under a separate screw terminal on the switch. Thus, operating the key switch opens and closes the circuit in the red wire.

Connect the wire ends from the switch loop to the

Security System Trouble-Shooting Chart

PROBLEMS	CAUSES	REPAIRS
Key switch turns alarm off, but alarm sounds immediately when key switch is turned on	1. Faulty connection in switching unit loop.	1. Check each terminal screw in loop for satisfactory connection. Also check loop connection to bell. Test system for satisfactory reset.
	2. Defect in switching unit.	2. Place jumper across the terminals of each switching unit, one at a time, to test the system. Satisfactory reset indicates that the jumped switching unit is defective. Replace defective unit.
	3. Faulty conductor in two-wire loop cable.	3. Replace loop cable. Test system for satisfactory reset.
	4. Fault in solid-state switching circuit.	4. Replace entire bell assembly.
Alarm will not sound when door or window is opened	1. Batteries weak or exhausted.	1. Replace batteries; or recharge old batteries, if possible.
	2. Defective key switch.	2. Place jumper across the terminals of the key switch; then trigger system by opening a door or window. If alarm does not sound, replace key switch.
	3. Defective solid-state switch.	3. Replace entire bell assembly.
False alarm occurs randomly	1. Door or window not fully closed.	1. Check to make sure doors and windows are fully closed.
	2. Loose connection in loop wiring.	2. Check each terminal location in loop. Jiggle wire at terminal to try to cause a false alarm. If alarm rings, repair loose connection.
	3. Faulty loop component.	3. Briskly tap each magnet switch and fire sensor. Replace unit that, when tapped, sets off false alarm.
	4. Defective solid-state switch.	4. Replace entire bell assembly.

two smaller wires (wires that are neither red or black) on the bell. Now fasten the bell to its backplate, and tighten the attachment screw. Finally, with the key switch in the "off" position, attach the short wire between the two battery cells.

Close all the entry-detection switches by shutting all windows and doors in the loop. Turn the key switch on. The circuit should now be in operation. Prove it by opening a door; the alarm should sound. Close the door, and the system should keep ringing. Turning off the key switch, however, should shut off the alarm. Turn the key switch back on; the alarm should remain off until the loop circuit is again interrupted.

If the alarm sounds as soon as you turn the key switch on, check the loop circuit to make sure that it is intact: All switches must be closed; all wires have to be attached properly to switches under terminal screws; no break can exist in the window foil. On the other hand, if the alarm does not sound when you open the door, check to make sure that the key is on and that the wiring from battery to bell is correct. In addition, make sure that the batteries are not exhausted.

Once you get the system into operation, set it off deliberately about once a week just to make certain that the circuit is still in good condition and that the batteries still contain enough power to operate the system properly. Test the system only briefly; then turn it off and reset if.

If you wish, you can leave the security system turned on (in the sentry mode, not with bell ringing) for a considerable period of time. Since the entry-detection switch circuit draws a standby current of only about a thousandth of an ampere, the batteries should last for months when used only to supply the entry-detection switch loop. Ringing the bell, though, puts a heavy drain on the batteries, after a few hours of ringing the bell, the batteries become exhausted and the bell stops ringing. Know how much use your batteries can stand, and replace or recharge them before their energy is depleted.

When you combine this intruder alarm system with a timer that switches on lights and a radio, you have a home security system that compares favorably with some of the most elaborate and expensive systems. Moreover, you have a security system that you can keep in good operating condition easily and at little expense.

INSTALLING A HOME INTERCOM SYSTEM

A home intercommunication system can be much more than just an easy way to call members of the family to dinner or to summon someone for a phone call. At relatively modest cost, you can have — in addition to a paging system — an intercom that includes a radio to provide music throughout the house. Moreover, you can enhance home security with a front-door speaker

Here Is What You Will Need

Materials

- Master intercom station
- Indoor substations
- Outdoor substation (optional)
- Intercom wire
- Miscellanous hardware (if required)

Tools

- Drill with bits
- Hammer (optional)
- Screwdrivers
- Electrician's diagonal cutters
- Stepladder (optional)
- Auxiliary light source (optional)
- Wire stripper
- Keyhole or saber saw
- Marking pencil
- Tape measure
- Scratch awl
- Torpedo level
- Utility knife
- Fish-wire or snake (optional)

that allows you to talk with a visitor before opening the door. Installing the system requires only moderate carpentry ability along with some relatively simple wiring tasks.

An intercom system has one major focal point — the master station. It contains the electronic circuitry for the voice communications — and, if it is a music system, the master station contains the radio. Some systems, in fact, include a combination AM-FM radio at the master station, and perhaps a tape player as well.

Intercom stations, at which you can only listen and reply, are called slave, remote or substations. The typical substation contains a speaker (which doubles as a microphone during reply) and a switch to transfer from "listen" to "talk" modes of operation. A typical installation consists of a master station installed at a convenient location, several indoor substations, and an outdoor substation. Usually, the outdoor substation is at the front door and includes the button for the doorbell or chimes.

In some intercom sets, all operations are controlled by the master station: power on/off, radio on/off, and call station selection. You can only call one substation at a time — or all at one time — from the master station, and only the single station you call can reply. Operating the push-to-talk button or lever, moreover, cuts off the sound of the radio for the duration of your conversation. More elaborate systems allow communication with or monitoring of any substation, call initiation from substation to substation or from substation to master station, or privacy at any substation without being monitored, plus music transmission to any or all substations.

All parts of the built-in system, even the master station, are sufficiently thin so that you can install them flush on a wall in holes cut into the wall space. The master station will usually fit in the space between wall studs. All wiring can be hidden; route it through the wall and alongside some of the underfloor joists. For example, suppose that you want to install a one-master, four-substation system. Although such a system would be adequate only for a small home, the same principles can be applied easily to a more extensive installation in a larger building.

Begin the installation by selecting the location for the master station, and then inspect the master station box or enclosure to determine how large an opening you must cut for it. Usually the manufacturer provides a bracket or flange, with holes for the mounting screws, for installing the master station within the wall. After you make the necessary measurements to determine the size and shape of hole for the master station and its mounting provisions, locate the studs inside the wall.

The hole you cut should be located between the studs. Decide on a convenient height above the floor — 5 feet is a good compromise for both short and tall persons — and pencil the shape of the master station hole on the wall. Drill ⅜-inch holes into the wall at the four corners of your pencilled outline, then use a keyhole or saber saw to cut out the hole for the master station. Set the master station box in place to make sure that it fits the hole, and trim the edges of the hole if necessary. Then set the box aside until you finish installing the wiring.

Cut similar holes in the walls at each substation location. Try the holes for size, trim as necessary, and then set the substations aside until after you install their wiring too.

Next, check your wiring diagram. In the usual master station-substation installation, only the master station connects to the household's electrical system. Multi-wire cable links the substations to the master station. If such cable is not supplied with the kit you buy or if you need additional cable, you can purchase it separately from a radio-electronics parts supplier. Ask for intercom cable with the required number of conductors, preferably with a jacket covering the conductors.

Run a separate cable from each substation back to

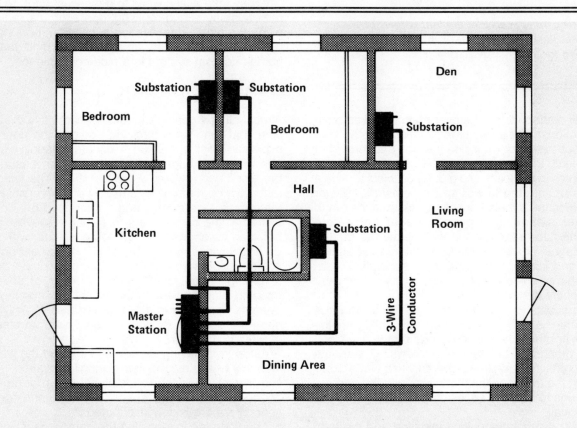

Begin the installation of the home intercom system by selecting the locations for the master station and substations. Often, the master station is located in the home's kitchen.

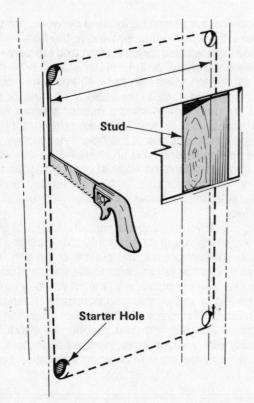

After drilling holes at each of the four corners of your pencilled outline, use a keyhole or saber saw to cut out the opening for your master station.

the master station (or in whatever manner indicated in the instructions). For a neater installation, run the wire from the substation down inside the wall and through a small hole into the basement area. Then, pass the wire through holes in the joists and alongside joists to a hole that leads up into the in-wall space below the master station. Since the cables from all the substations run to the master station, you need a larger entry hole through the floor space in the wall below the master station. Maneuver each cable up to the master station opening, and label it according to its substation location. Numbered pieces of pressure-sensitive tape work well to identify the wires.

At each substation location, connect the three wires to the terminals on the substation unit, following the wire color or other identification code that you will find stamped alongside the terminal screws. Fasten the substation unit in the wall — preferably to a wall stud — and attach the trim molding that surrounds the perimeter of the unit to hide the edges of the opening that you cut in the wall.

With all the substation wiring installed and the substations themselves mounted in the wall, it is time to run line power to the master station. **Caution:** If you

have a master station that connects directly to your home's electrical system, be sure to deenergize the circuit involved and to take precautions to prevent someone else from turning it back on while you are working on the circuit. If a transformer is supplied with the master station to power the system, locate the transformer on or near a junction box or the main entrance panel, and connect it to the electrical system (after you deenergize the circuit) according to the manufacturer's instructions

Finally, attach all substation and power line wires to the master station, but be sure that you make the attachments according to the markings on the master station's terminal connections. Mount the master station in the wall, affix it firmly to the wall studs, and attach the trim molding. Then restore power to the circuit.

Once you have the system installed, test it to see how well it performs. If any one of the substations fails to work, check the connections to its terminals as well as the connections that its wires make to the master station. If you suspect a defective substation unit, interchange it with another. That should isolate the problem either to wiring defects or to a defective unit, thereby allowing you to make the necessary repairs.

It may take a little while to get accustomed to calling remote stations and replying, operating the radio, and using the caller-identification substation; but once you use the system a few times, you will find that your home intercom system is a nice convenience.

GARAGE DOOR OPENER

Almost all garages built in recent years have the kind of door that runs on a track that guides the door to an overhead position. Since a counterbalance or spring bears the main burden of raising the door, it usually can be raised and lowered with little effort. The typical garage door opener consists mainly of a reversible motor that drives a carriage along a rail above the door. Attached to the carriage is a drawbar to move the door between its opened and closed positions, with travel-limiting devices to stop the door's movement precisely at the fully opened and fully closed positions. A relay or reversing switch reverses the direction of drive from opening to closing and back again. Deluxe garage door openers feature a radio receiver that allows you to open the door by sending a signal from an electronic module in your car.

Aside from having to hoist and support the weight of the fairly heavy mechanism during installation, you will find it relatively easy to install your own garage door opener. Kits that are specifically designed for do-it-yourselfers are widely distributed.

The first step in installing the garage door opener is to determine the location for the mechanism. Use a folding rule or tape to measure the width of the garage

Intercom Trouble-Shooting Chart

PROBLEMS	CAUSES	REPAIRS
System totally inoperative	1. Blown fuse or tripped circuit breaker; loose line connection, break in power circuit.	1. Inspect load center. Replace fuse or reset circuit breaker. Check power circuit and connections.
	2. Defective transformer. Output can be tested with a voltmeter.	2. Replace with new transformer of same power rating and voltage step-down ratio.
	3. Defect in master station.	3. Replace master station.
One substation only inoperative	1. Defective wiring to substation.	1. Verify wiring fault by temporarily interchanging inoperative substation with substation that operates satisfactorily. Replace intercom wiring to inoperative substation location.
	2. Defective substation.	2. Verify substation defect by interchanging. Replace defective unit.
	3. Defective selector switch in master station or other internal problem.	3. Repair master station.
Station can receive voice call, but cannot reply	1. Faulty "talk-listen" switch in substation.	1. Replace switch in substation or replace substation, whichever is more feasible.
	2. Faulty wiring to substation.	2. Verify wiring fault by temporarily interchanging inoperative substation with substation that operates satisfactorily. Replace intercom wiring to inoperative substation location.
Radio reception is erratic or totally inoperative at all substations, although voice calls can be sent and received	1. Faulty radio in master station.	2. Replace or repair radio unit or replace master station.

door. Half this distance is the center of the door. On the inside of the door, toward the top, draw a short vertical line down the center of the door. When you affix the drawbar (the mechanism for raising and lowering the door) at this line, the door weight will be evenly balanced at the lifting point.

Raise and lower the door, and observe the top point of its travel. Mark this location because you must mount the opener so that the rail is higher than the peak of the door's travel. Otherwise, as the door opens, it could strike the rail.

The door opener must be affixed to the garage at two points: above the motor drive unit and at the outer end of the rail. Inspect the area right above the garage door at your vertical dividing line; there must be a support member in that location suitable for attaching the front end of the rail. If your garage lacks a structural member in that location, your first step in installing the door opener is to obtain a front mounting board. Center and fasten a length of 2x6-inch plank securely with lag screws across two wall studs over your mark of highest door travel. Transfer your high-point mark to this plank, and extend the vertical door center line that you drew earlier onto the plank.

Here Is What You Will Need

Materials

- Garage door opener kit
- Mounting brackets
- Length of 2″ x 6″ plank (optional)
- Length of 2″ x 4″ stock (optional)
- ¾″ plywood panel (optional)
- Miscellaneous hardware (as required)

Tools

- Screwdrivers
- Hammer
- Saw
- Wrenches
- Drill with bits
- Tape measure
- Marking pencil
- Electrician's diagonal cutters
- Two stepladders
- Auxiliary light source (optional)
- Extension cord
- Scratch awl

The next phase of the installation must be done with the door down, so if there are no lights in the garage you will need an auxiliary light source to see what you are doing. Much of the work, moreover, must be done from a stepladder. Although the job can be done by one person, you really should have someone assist you throughout the installation. The person will also require a stepladder.

Assemble the rail to the motor unit on the garage floor, following the procedure outlined in the kit instructions. With the garage door down, lift and fasten the outermost end of the rail to the front mounting plank at a location about 2 inches above the intersecting marks you made for your door's high point and center line. Usually, the rail bracket provided for this purpose fastens to the front mounting plank by lag screws. If bolts and nuts are provided, however, you must drill suitable holes through the front mounting plank. Be sure to use washers under the heads of the bolts to keep them from pressing into the wood.

Raise the motor assembly to the point where the rail is horizontal, or parallel with the door track. With the motor assembly held or supported in this position, raise and lower the garage door by hand to make sure that the rail location does not interfere with the door's

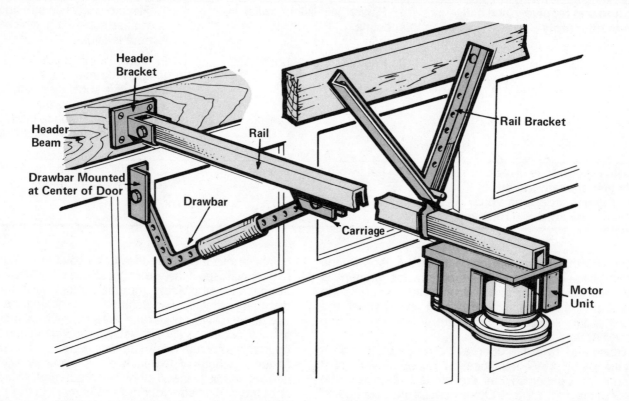

The typical garage door opener consists mainly of a reversible motor that drives a carriage along a rail above the door. Attached to the carriage is a drawbar to move the door between its opened and closed positions.

movement. Once you establish the correct position and height for the motor assembly, fasten it to the garage joists with the metal brackets in the kit. If the position of the motor assembly is between two joists, or if the garage joists run the same direction as the rail, you must fasten a length of 2x4 across the joists, and then mount the brackets to the 2x4. If your garage ceiling is finished, you can mount a ¾-inch plywood panel overhead — fastening it to the joists with lag screws — and attach the mounting hardware to the plywood panel with heavy-duty toggle bolts.

Attach the drawbar to the rail carriage, and move the carriage to its closed-door position. Mark the drawbar mounting-screw holes on the garage door, and drill the

Garage Door Opener Trouble-Shooting Chart

PROBLEMS	CAUSES	REPAIRS
Garage door opener totally inoperative	1. No line power.	1. Test garage receptacle with a different appliance for power. Check for blown fuse or tripped circuit breaker. Make necessary replacement or repairs.
	2. Defective motor.	2. Repair or replace motor.
	3. Motor overload tripped.	3. Reset or wait for automatic reset; check and remedy cause of overload.
Motor hums, but opener will not operate	1. Defective limit reversal operation.	1. Inspect trip mechanism for binding or broken parts. Repair or replace needed parts: relay or switch.
	2. Defective motor capacitor.	2. Replace capacitor.
	3. Damage in carriage drive.	3. Inspect for damage. Make suitable repairs.
Motor runs, but door opener will not operate	1. Broken belt or coupling.	1. Replace belt or coupling.
	2. Broken chain or worm drive.	2. Replace chain or repair worm drive.
	3. Loose set screw on drive pulley.	3. Tighten set screw.
Door operates from radio module, but not from push button	1. Defective push button.	1. Replace push button.
	2. Defective wiring.	2. Repair wiring to push button.
Door operates from push button, but not from radio module	1. Defective receiver.	1. Repair or replace receiver.
	2. Defective module.	2. Repair or replace module.
Door does not completely open or completely close	1. Incorrect adjustment of limit control device.	1. Adjust the limit control device according to kit instruction.
	2. Door binding.	2. Uncouple door from drawbar. Raise and lower by hand to verify binding. Correct as necessary.
Unit does not shut off when door meets an obstruction; e.g. rock, snow, etc.	1. Safety limit mechanism inoperative.	1. Inspect unit to determine how safety limit action occurs. Look for a defective component or an incorrect adjustment. Make necessary repairs or adjustments.

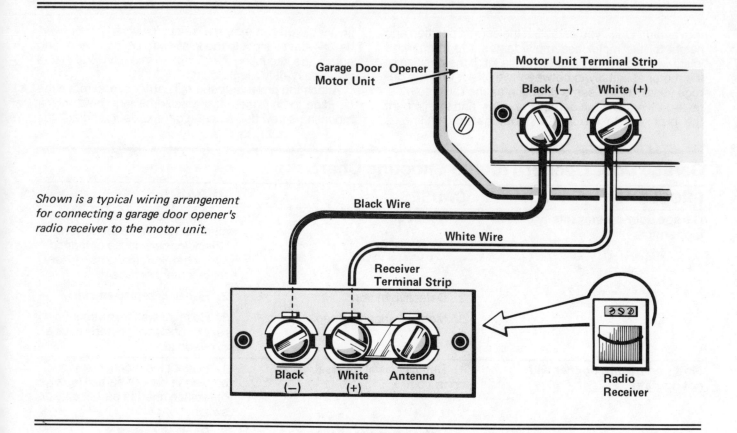

Motor Unit Terminal Strip

Garage Door Opener Motor Unit

Black (−)   White (+)

Shown is a typical wiring arrangement for connecting a garage door opener's radio receiver to the motor unit.

Black Wire

White Wire

Receiver Terminal Strip

Black (−)   White (+)   Antenna

Radio Receiver

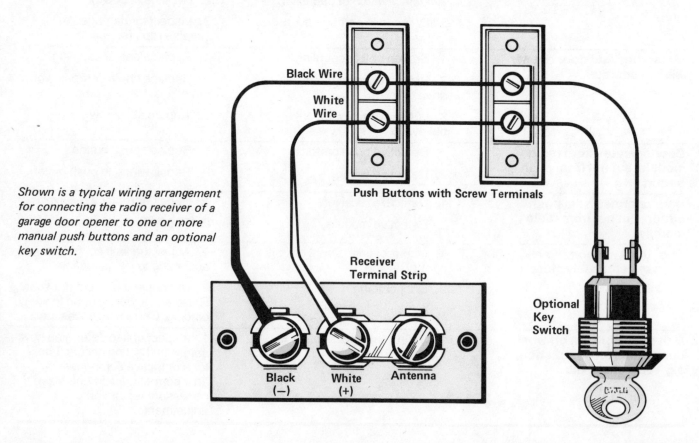

Black Wire

White Wire

Push Buttons with Screw Terminals

Shown is a typical wiring arrangement for connecting the radio receiver of a garage door opener to one or more manual push buttons and an optional key switch.

Receiver Terminal Strip

Black (−)   White (+)   Antenna

Optional Key Switch

holes in the door. With the drawbar mounted and the holes drilled, insert and tighten the attaching hardware that fastens the drawbar to the door.

Now, make all the necessary adjustments to the drive chain or lead screw, observing particularly the location of the travel-limit cams. You must understand just how these cams cause the device to turn off automatically at the "Door-open" and "Door-closed" positions, and how they make the motor reverse its direction and rotation. Install the radio receiver and manual push button. You can use ordinary bell wire for the push button, but be sure to locate it in a place where you can see the garage door opener in operation when you push the button.

Plug the drive assembly cord into an extension cord, and plug the extension cord into a convenient receptacle. Set the garage door in motion, using the manual push button. During the door's first test rising, pull the plug from the extension cord several times so you can check to make sure that there is no binding anywhere and that the lifting action is satisfactory. Make any necessary corrections using the adjustment provisions built into the garage door-opener system, and verify the operation of the radio remote module.

Once you feel confident that the garage door opener is operating properly, disconnect the extension cord, and plug the drive assembly line cord into its permanent outlet. If possible, connect the cord to the garage overhead light socket. A pull-chain adapter then allows you to deenergize the garage door opener whenever you will not be using it for an extended period or when the unit needs servicing.

WIRING YOUR HOME FOR SOUND

Have you ever wished that you could have music from your stereophonic sound system follow you throughout the house wherever you go? Perhaps you have been told that you can only make your wish come true if your sound system is especially engineered to accommodate extra speakers. Basically, that is true, but there is one speaker arrangement that is so simple that no special engineering is required. Best of all, do-it-yourself installation of this speaker system is easy.

Here is the problem: The typical home sound system has two speakers, one for each stereo channel. When you simply hook on additional speakers, you create an impedance mis-match, which not only degrades the tone quality but also may damage the electronic parts of your sound system. It is the impedance mis-match that has fostered the blanket rule not to add more speakers to your system.

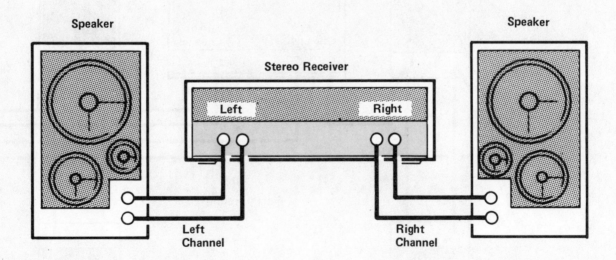

The typical home stereo system has two speakers—one for each stereo channel—and adding a speaker or two will result in impedance mis-match and degraded sound quality. However, it is possible to obtain acceptable stereo sound throughout your home by adding three pairs of speakers to your present system by using series-parallel circuitry.

Here Is What You Will Need

Materials

- Length of Type SPT #16 gauge cord (or speaker cable)
- 6 extension speakers (to match impedance of existing pair)
- Miscellaneous hardware
- Staples for Type SPT cord (or other, as required)
- Solderless connectors (as required)

Tools

- Drill with bits
- Screwdrivers (optional)
- Wire stripper
- Electrician's diagonal cutters
- Fish-wire or snake (optional)
- Tape measure (optional)
- Marking pencil (optional)

Look at the rear of your stereo, and you will probably see two connections for the left channel and two for the right channel. One speaker is wired to the terminals for the left-channel output, and the other speaker is wired to the right-channel output. In high-quality stereos, each speaker is actually a combination of two or more speaker units — possibly a large-diameter woofer for low sounds and a small-diameter tweeter for high sounds. The two units work together as a single wide-range speaker combination. Nevertheless, even in such units, all speaker leads connect back to the two-conductor cable between the speaker and the tuner-amplifier.

Two important speaker specifications — the watts and the ohms — are imprinted somewhere, either on the speaker itself or on an attached label. The wattage rating tells you how much sound power — loudness — the speaker can handle without damage. If your amplifier can deliver 60 watts, your speakers must be capable of handling that much power. Too much power to a speaker is called "overdriving" and results in distortion, while severe overdriving of a speaker can damage it.

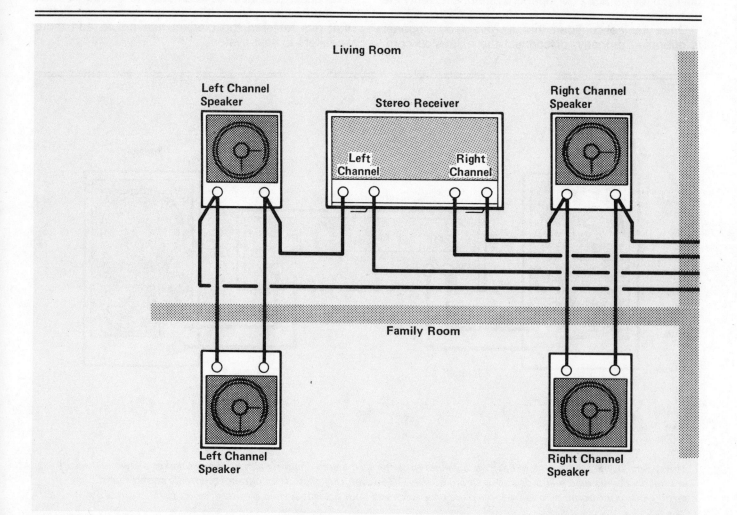

Even more important are the speaker ohms specification. Most systems are engineered for 8-ohm speakers, and most speakers sold today are 8-ohm speakers. Connecting a second speaker to either channel results in unbalanced ohms — or impedance mis-match — and the sound performance is degraded.

It is possible, nonetheless, to connect four speakers to one channel in an unusual wiring arrangement. With this particular wiring, four 8-ohm speakers act like one 8-ohm speaker. There is, however, some loss of sound quality, but your system will not be harmed. The arrangement is known as a series-parallel circuit, and with it you can install a pair of speakers in four different locations (total of 8 speakers). For example, you could install a pair of speakers in four rooms in your home, three rooms plus the patio or two rooms upstairs and two rooms downstairs. Any combination of four locations will work, but it must be four — and only four — speakers on each channel, wired together for each channel and expanded to two channels.

Although the only absolute requirement for all speakers is that they must have the same impedance

— usually 8 ohms each — you will be more satisfied with the results if all speakers are the same model from the same manufacturer. Unless you are prepared to do some cabinetmaking, you should purchase speakers that are already mounted in suitable enclosures. If you wish to conceal the speakers in a piece of furniture or to build enclosures that fit a certain space, however, you should buy unmounted speakers of a quality comparable to the performance of those of your stereo system.

Lamp cord, Type SPT, in #16 gauge, is quite suitable for wiring the tuner-amplifier in your stereo to the extension speakers. Or you may use a 2-conductor speaker cable. To keep the installation neat, route the extension wiring inside the walls or through the under-floor space. Unlike wiring for lights and receptacles, the speaker wire can run through small holes (5/16-inch diameter). Drill the floor hole near a corner where it will be inconspicuous, and run the wire to the hole along the baseboard. Dark-colored cord is recommended because you can run it along a dark-painted baseboard in a manner that makes it almost unnoticeable. Of

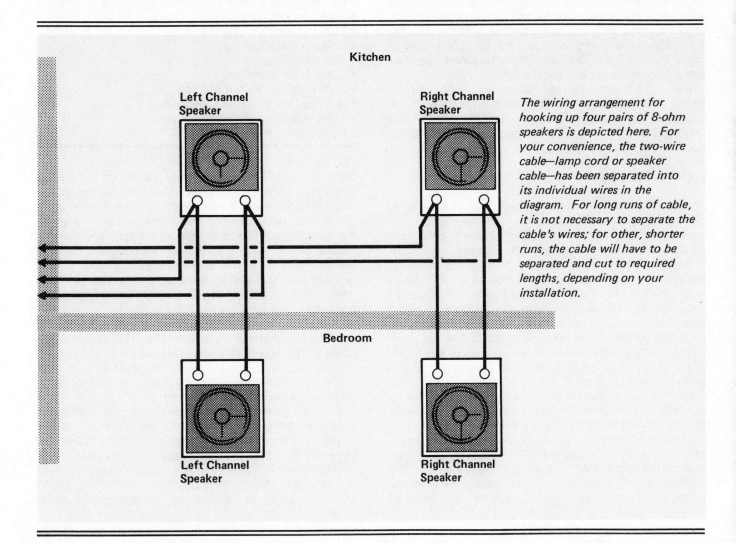

Kitchen

Left Channel Speaker

Right Channel Speaker

The wiring arrangement for hooking up four pairs of 8-ohm speakers is depicted here. For your convenience, the two-wire cable—lamp cord or speaker cable—has been separated into its individual wires in the diagram. For long runs of cable, it is not necessary to separate the cable's wires; for other, shorter runs, the cable will have to be separated and cut to required lengths, depending on your installation.

Bedroom

Left Channel Speaker

Right Channel Speaker

course, if your baseboards are white, use white cord. If all your wiring will be hidden inside the walls or in the underfloor space, though, then consider using a different color cord for each channel. The different colors will help you install the wiring correctly. Drive small staples into the baseboards about every 3 feet of the run and at the corners to keep the installation neat, but be careful you do not damage the wire.

As far as the wiring itself is concerned, follow the accompanying diagram to hook up the four pairs of speakers. After you have completed the wiring for all the speakers, turn on the system. If one channel fails to operate properly, turn off the system immediately and determine the cause of trouble. In the four-speaker wiring circuit, a poor connection to any one speaker (or one faulty speaker) affects the entire channel, causing an imbalance in sound output.

BUILT-IN APPLIANCES

When built-in appliances are mentioned, you usually think of the food waste disposer, the countertop range, and the dishwasher. Of course, two of these — the range and the dishwasher — are also available in portable versions that you can remove and replace by doing little more than unplugging the appliance. Servicing or installing a built-in appliance, however, requires some knowledge of electrical wiring.

If you are installing a new built-in appliance, you will find it advisable first to determine the location where you want the appliance, then to run the wiring, and finally, after the wiring is in, to position the appliance and connect the wiring.

Food Waste Disposer

The first step in servicing any built-in appliance is to disconnect it from the power line. In the case of the food waste disposer, all you should have to do is turn off the wall switch. However, in the interest of safety, it is preferable to disconnect the power for the circuit at the main entrance panel. Now look at the electrical wiring that connects your disposer to your home's electrical system. You will see Type NM cable or a flexible steel cable coming out from within the wall or a wall-mounted junction box and attaching to the disposer wiring inside an enclosure on the bottom of the appliance. If you loosen one or more of the enclosure screws, you can open it.

Ordinarily, the electrical connections consist simply of black wire in cable to black wire in appliance, white wire to white wire, and bare or ground wire to a special grounding terminal or, in lieu of that, under any available screw that provides a suitable ground to the metal body of the appliance. Disconnect the wires, loosen the connector, and take out the line cable. Then, screw solderless connectors (wirenuts) on the bare ends of

Here Is What You Will Need

Materials

- Appliance(s)
- Type NM cable (or other cable, as required)
- Solderless connectors
- Staples for Type NM cable (or other, as required)
- Circuit breaker (optional)
- Cable clamps (as required)
- Single-pole toggle switch and box (for disposer)
- Miscellaneous hardware (as required)
- Electrical tape (optional)

Tools

- Screwdrivers
- Hammer (optional)
- Electrician's diagonal cutters
- Stepladder (optional)
- Auxiliary light source (optional)
- Keyhole or saber saw (optional)
- Drill with bits (optional)
- Wire stripper (optional)
- Marking pencil (optional)
- Scratch awl (optional)
- Pliers (optional)
- Utility knife (optional)
- Fish-wire or snake (optional)
- Armored cable cutter (optional)
- Tape measure (optional)
- Punch (optional)

each line cable wire to provide insulation protection while you service the appliance. After you repair the disposer (or obtain a replacement if the appliance is beyond repair), reposition the disposer, fasten it under the sink, attach the cable the same way it was connected before and replace the bottom cover. Turn on the power in the circuit and test the disposer.

If you plan to install a new food waste disposer, you must make sure that there is a spare branch circuit in your main entrance panel. If no spare circuit is available for the new built-in appliance, you will have to install a 20-ampere circuit breaker. Obtain enough cable (Type NM #12-2 with ground or other type as necessary) for a run from the appliance to a wall switch, and from the switch all the way back to the main fuse box or circuit breaker panel.

You will need to make openings in the wall for a switch near the disposer and for the cable run to the disposer. Plan the installation so that both holes are between the same two wall studs. From the basement or attic space — whichever is more accessible in your home — drill a third hole in a location that allows you to feed the cable into the wall (again between the same

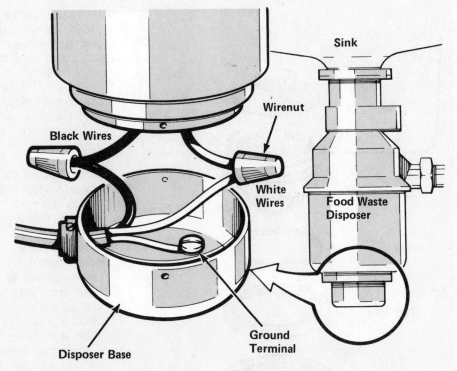

Ordinarily, the electrical connections in a food waste disposer consist of black wire in cable to black appliance wire, white wire in cable to white appliance wire, and a bare or ground wire to a special grounding terminal or available screw that provides a suitable ground to the metal body of the unit.

Black Wires

Wirenut

White Wires

Food Waste Disposer

Sink

Disposer Base

Ground Terminal

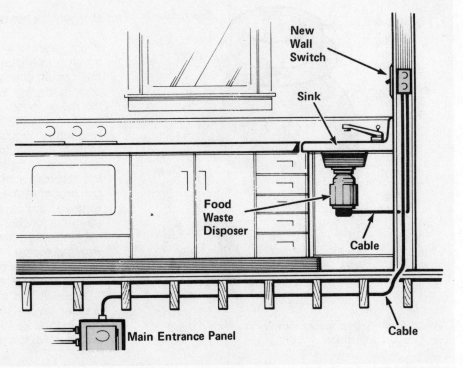

To install a new food waste disposer, you will have to make an opening in the wall for a switch near the disposer and for the cable run to the disposer, and be able to run the cable for the new branch circuit to the main entrance panel.

New Wall Switch

Sink

Food Waste Disposer

Cable

Cable

Main Entrance Panel

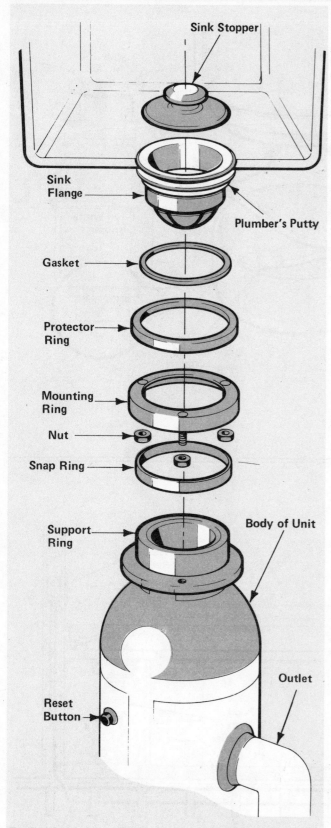

Sink Stopper

Sink Flange

Plumber's Putty

Gasket

Protector Ring

Mounting Ring

Nut

Snap Ring

Support Ring

Body of Unit

Outlet

Reset Button

Typical food waste disposer showing standard fittings and installation location.

two studs as the switch opening). Fish the cable into the inside wall space and out through the hole for the switch. Then, feed the cable through and alongside the joists and back to the main panel by the most convenient route.

Run another length of cable through the wall from the switch opening out through the hole near the disposer. At the location where you will install a single-pole toggle switch, run both cable ends into a switch box, tighten the cable clamps, and mount the box in the wall — preferably to a wall stud, but otherwise with plaster clips. Follow the procedure outlined in the section "New Lighting Fixtures" describing how to install a new switch box and switch.

Mount the disposer to the sink according to the manufacturer's instructions. With the disposer's bottom cover removed, connect the cable from the new disposer switch to the disposer and replace the bottom cover. Ordinarily, the electrical connections are as follows: black wire to black wire, white wire to white wire, and bare or ground wire to a special grounding terminal or, in lieu of that, under any available screw that provides a suitable ground to the metal of the disposer.

Caution: Deenergize the main entrance panel by turning off the main disconnect to cut the current throughout your home. Install a new circuit breaker in the panel by following the procedure outlined in the section "Adding a Branch Circuit." With the new circuit breaker installed and circuit wires connected, turn on the main disconnect. Then turn on the new circuit breaker. Go back to the new wall switch and see whether your new food waste disposer operates as it should.

Built-In Dishwasher

If you plan to work on your built-in dishwasher, you must deenergize the appropriate branch circuit. Use the circuit directory inside the main entrance panel door to identify the fuse or circuit breaker that controls the dishwasher circuit. If you want to service the dishwasher with the appliance remaining in place, it is not necessary to disconnect the dishwasher line wires. Most of the electrical parts — motor, relay, water valve, and timer — have lead wires that you can detach from the remainder of the circuit to allow removal and replacement of the defective components. If you plan to remove and replace the entire appliance, however, open the junction box on the appliance and detach the cable in a manner similar to that described for the food waste disposer. After you service the dishwasher, turn the power back on by attaching the line wires and restoring the fuse or turning the circuit breaker on.

You will find that the installation of a built-in dishwasher involves much the same kind of wiring as the built-in food waste disposer, except that there is no wall switch. With the dishwasher away from its final mount-

If you plan to work on your built-in dishwasher, you must deenergize the appropriate branch circuit. If you plan to service the appliance in place, it is not necessary to disconnect its line wires. Most of the electrical parts have lead wires that you can detach from the remainder of the circuit to allow removal and replacement of defective components.

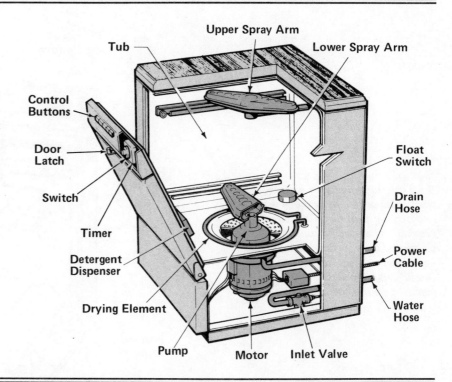

Tub — Upper Spray Arm — Lower Spray Arm — Control Buttons — Door Latch — Switch — Timer — Detergent Dispenser — Drying Element — Pump — Motor — Inlet Valve — Water Hose — Power Cable — Drain Hose — Float Switch

ing location, drill a hole in the wall or in the floor space, and run a length of cable (Type NM #12-2, with ground, or other as required) back to the main entrance panel. Attach the cable to an existing or newly installed 20-ampere circuit breaker or a fuse socket. **Caution:** If you connect the new dishwasher to an existing circuit, make sure that a current overload does not result.

Move the dishwasher into place, and attach the cable to the dishwasher wiring following the diagram attached inside the appliance. With the dishwasher timer turned to "off," put in the fuse or turn on the circuit breaker to energize the circuit. That completes the installation, and you can now try the dishwasher. It is not necessary to run the appliance through its entire cycle, however. Simply advance the control knob to the various positions, leaving the knob in each position only long enough to verify that each function — rinse, wash, dry — operates properly.

Built-In Electric Range

If you are planning to install a built-in range, first make sure that your home has 220-240-volt service. You must either have or install a double-pole circuit breaker of from 30-ampere size on up, depending on the range load. To install the circuit breaker and to make the electrical connections in the main panel, follow the procedure described in the section "Installing a 220-240-Volt Receptacle." If your main panel does not have the capacity for this added load, you may need to have an electrician install an additional circuit breaker box just

for your new electric range.

Run a cable (size depends on range load, type of code requirements, and particular wiring conditions) from the main panel to the location of the built-in range. At the range, use the wiring diagram supplied with the built-in surface unit and oven units as a guide. Although the internal wiring of the range may seem complex, you need only connect the cable's three wires plus ground under the terminal screws or to the similar-colored conductors from the range wiring.

With all surface-unit and oven switches in the "off" position, energize the newly installed range circuitry by turning on the circuit breaker; then, verify your installation by testing each surface element and each oven element. If each one heats as it should, then you know that you installed your new built-in range properly.

Built-in countertop ranges usually have flexible metallic conduit over the wire that extends back to an electrical junction box behind the range. From this point, the wire is routed to the controllers and heating elements. Rarely is it necessary to disconnect the cable to service the range. Repairs generally consist of replacing a faulty switch assembly, an inoperative thermostatic controller or a defective heating element. **Caution:** Before making any of these repairs, be sure to deenergize the range circuit by removing fuses or turning off the circuit breaker. Since it is fed by a three-wire circuit, the range is energized through two fuses or a double-pole circuit breaker. Unless the fuses or circuit breaker are deenergized, the range is not safe to work on.

Once you have installed your built-in electric range, energize the new range circuitry by turning on the circuit breaker. Then verify your installation by testing each surface element and each oven element. If each heats as it should, you know that you have installed your electric range properly.

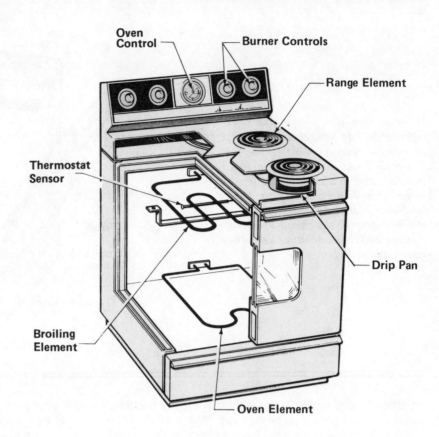

Oven Control

Burner Controls

Range Element

Thermostat Sensor

Drip Pan

Broiling Element

Oven Element

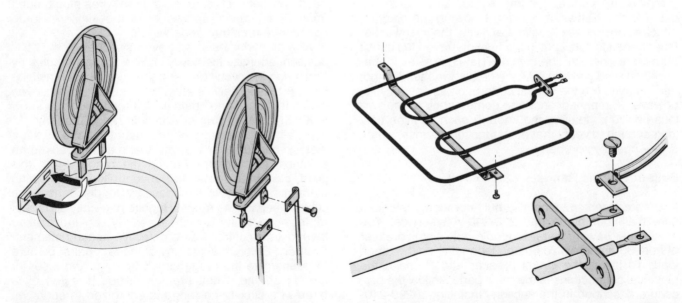

The surface elements of an electric range can generally be replaced quite easily. They either plug in (left) or are attached with screws.

To remove a faulty oven or broiler element from an electric range, loosen the mounting screws, pull the unit forward, and disconnect the wiring.

Glossary

A

AC Cable: A type of metal-clad cable used in residential branch-circuit wiring.

Alternating Current (AC): An electric current that reverses its direction at regular intervals.

Ammeter: An instrument for measuring the amount of electron flow (current) in amperes.

Ampacity: The current-carrying capacity of electric conductors, expressed in amperes.

Ampere: The practical mks (meter-kilogram-second) unit of electric current, equivalent to a steady current produced by the application of 1 volt across a resistance of 1 ohm.

Appliance: Utilization equipment normally built in standardized sizes and types, usually other than industrial, designed, installed and connected to perform one or more specific work functions, such as food-mixing, cooking, clothes washing, etc.

B

Ballast: A magnetic coil that adjusts current flow through a fluorescent lamp, providing the necessary current surge to start the lamp, and maintaining an even flow of current for continuous operation of the lamp.

Battery: A combination of two or more galvanic cells electrically connected to work together to produce electricity.

Branch Circuit: Circuit conductors running between the final overcurrent protection device on the circuit and the outlets.

Breaker Points: Metal contacts that open and close a circuit at timed intervals.

Bus: A rigid conductor in an electric circuit, often in the shape of a bar, used to connect three or more circuits.

BX Cable: An outmoded type of metal-clad cable once widely used in wiring residential and other branch circuits.

C

Cable: A solid or stranded single conductor, or a combination of conductors insulated from one another and enclosed in a single jacket.

Circuit: The complete path of an electric current.

Circuit Breaker: An electromagnetic or thermal overcurrent protection device that opens a circuit when the current in the circuit exceeds a predetermined level. The device can be reset.

Closed Circuit: An uninterrupted circuit forming a path through which current can flow.

Conductivity: The ability of a given substance to conduct electric current.

Conductor: Any material capable of conducting or transmitting electric current.

Conduit: Special pipe, usually made of galvanized steel or aluminum and properly called rigid metallic conduit, made expressly for containing electrical wires and cables.

Conduit Body: A separate part of a tubing or conduit system that allows access by means of one or more removable covers or plates to the enclosed wires at either a junction of two or more conduit sections or at a terminal point.

Continuity: The condition of being continuous, with uninterrupted current flow or unbroken connection.

Convenience Outlet: A point of utilization in a wiring system, generally taken to mean a duplex receptacle.

Current: The movement or flow of electricity along or through a conductor.

D

Device: An electrical component that carries current but does not use it, like a switch or receptacle.

Direct Current (DC): An electric current of constant direction and essentially constant magnitude.

Disconnect: A device or group of devices that can be manipulated to disconnect the conductors of a circuit from their supply source.

Duplex: Term given to a duplex receptacle, or two receptacles molded as one unit.

E

Efficiency: The ratio of output power to input power, generally expressed as a percentage.

Electromotive Force: The potential difference between the terminals of a source of electrical energy, expressed in volts.

EMT: Electrical metallic tubing, or "thinwall," made especially to contain electrical wires and cables.

Enclosure: Any approved box-like unit made to house or protect electrical devices, equipment, and connections.

F

Feeder Circuit: Circuit conductors running from service equipment to branch circuit overcurrent protection device.

Frequency: The number of complete cycles per second existing in any form of wave motion, such as the number of cycles per second of an alternating current.

Fuse: An overcurrent protection device inserted in series with a circuit. It contains a metal that will melt or break when current is increased beyond a specific value for a definite period of time.

G

GFI: Ground fault interrupter, a special type of overcurrent protection device that also detects current leakage in a circuit and guards against shock hazard.

Ground: A metallic connection with the earth to establish ground potential.

Grounded Wiring Systems: Those in which all metal enclosures, cable armor, devices, fixtures and all exposed metallic parts of the wiring system are linked together through the equipment grounding circuit and ultimately connected to the grounding bus of the main entrance panel, and to earth through the grounding electrode.

Grounding Electrode: A heavy conductor or a network of conductors, usually buried in the earth, that provides a low-impedance path between electrical equipment or circuitry and earth.

H

Hertz: A unit of frequency equal to 1 cycle per second.

Home Run: The part of an electrical circuit between the last overcurrent protection device on the circuit and the first outlet.

Horsepower: The English unit of power that is equal to work done at the rate of 550 foot-pounds per second; equal to 746 watts of electrical power.

Hot Wire: The conductor in a cable that carries the current, or load; a live or energized conductor or cable.

HPD Cable: Cloth-covered, asbestos-filled cord used on heat-producing, high-current draw appliances.

HPN Cable: Heat-resistant thermoplastic-insulated cord used on heat-producing, high-current draw appliances.

I

Impedance: The total opposition to current flow in an alternating-current circuit.

K

Kilo-: A prefix meaning 1,000.

Kilowatt: A unit of electrical power equal to 1,000 watts.

Kilowatt-hour: A unit of electrical energy equal to the amount of energy expanded or transferred in 1 hour by 1 kilowatt of power.

L

Line Side: The contacts or terminals of an electrical device or equipment that are connected to a power source; the input.

Line Voltage: The specific voltage carried by a particular electrical line or circuit source.

Load: The electrical demand placed on a circuit or a system by the equipment connected to it; the electrical rating of required power or power consumption of any given piece of electrical equipment.

Load Side: The contacts or terminals of an electrical device or equipment that are connected to conductors carrying electricity away from the unit to other equipment or devices; the output.

M

Main Disconnect: The means provided to disconnect an entire electrical system from its source of supply.

Main Entrance Panel: A single approved enclosure that houses a main disconnect, main overcurrent protection devices, branch circuit overcurrent protection devices, and branch and feeder circuit distribution means.

Micro-: A prefix meaning one-millionth.

Milli-: A prefix meaning one-thousandth.

mks: Meter-kilogram-second, a system of unit measuring.

N

National Electrical Code (NEC): A set of guidelines for the installation of electrical systems, with the purpose of safeguarding persons and property from the hazards of electricity; adopted by many governmental bodies for exercising legal jurisdiction over electrical installations.

Negative Charge: The electrical charge carried by a body which has an excess of electrons.

Neutral: The wire or conductor in a cable that does not carry current unless and until the circuit is completed, or that carries the imbalance of current in a three-wire circuit.

NM Cable: A type of nonmetallic, plastic-sheathed cable widely used today in the wiring of residential branch circuits.

O

Ohm: The mks unit of resistance, equal to the resistance in a conductor in which 1 volt of potential difference produces a current of 1 ampere.

Ohmmeter: An instrument for directly measuring resistance in ohms.

Open Circuit: A discontinuous electrical circuit or path through which no current can flow.

Outlet: Any point in the wiring system at which current is taken to supply utilization equipment.

Overload: A load greater than the rated load or capacity of an electrical device, conductor or equipment.

Overload Protection Device: Properly called overcurrent protection device; a device designed to open an electrical circuit at a preset overcurrent level.

P

Polarity: The particular state, either positive or negative, with reference to the two poles, or electrification.

Pole: The section of a magnet where the flux lines are concentrated; also where they enter and leave the magnet; also, an electrode of a battery.

Positive Charge: The electrical charge carried by a body that has become deficient in electrons.

Potential Difference: The amount of charge held by a body as compared to another point or body, usually measured in volts.

Power: The rate of doing work or expending energy; measured and expressed in watts in the mks system.

Primary: Relating to or constituting the inducing current or its circuit in an induction coil or transformer.

R

Receptacle: A contact device installed at an electrical outlet for connection of a single attachment plug, through which current passes to power an electrical appliance or other equipment.

Relay: An electromechanical switching device that can be used as a remote control.

Resistance: A property of any given conductor that opposes the flow of current, equal to the voltage across the source divided by the current flow and measured in ohms.

S

Secondary: Relating to the induced current or its circuit in an inductance coil or transformer.

Series-Parallel Circuit: An electrical circuit in which some of the loads are connected in series with the poles of the source voltage and others are connected in parallel, in any combination.

Service: The entire combination of equipment and conductors needed to deliver electricity from the supply system to the wiring system of the served building or premises.

Service Drop: The overhead service conductors running from the last power pole to the connection point at the service-entrance conductors of the building or premises being served.

Service Equipment: The apparatus and equipment, such as circuit breaker, fuses or switch, located at or near the point of entrance of the service-entrance conductors into the building or premises, that serve as the means of disconnect of the supply.

Service Lateral: Underground service conductors running from the source of supply to the point of connection with the service-entrance conductors of the building or premises being served.

Short Circuit: An abnormal and generally unintentional condition of relatively low resistance between two points of different potential in a circuit that results in an excessive current flow.

SJ Cable: A type of cord having conductors insulated with rubber and encased in a rubber jacket, called Junior Hard Service Cord and approved for hard usage, employed as cords on nonheat-producing appliances, tools, and equipment.

SJT Cable: Similar to SJ cable, but with conductors insulated with either rubber or thermoplastic and an outer jacket of thermoplastic.

Solderless Connector: Terminal ends of various configurations that crimp onto wire ends and join with mating connectors on other conductors or electrical utilization equipment; insulating-body screw-on devices called wirenuts used to join two or more wires in electrical applications.

Solenoid: An electromagnetic coil that contains a movable plunger.

SP Cable: A type of cord having conductors insulated with rubber and contained in a rubber jacket, called All Rubber Parallel Cord, available in three types for various purposes and conditions: SP-1, SP-2, and SP-3. Not approved for hard usage; generally employed for wiring portable and pendant lighting fixtures and lamps.

SPT Cable: Similar to SP cable, but having conductors insulated with thermoplastic and enclosed in a thermoplastic jacket, called All Plastic Parallel Cord; often called "zip cord."

Starter: An automatic switch that opens (turns off) once current is flowing through a fluorescent lamp and the operating circuit has been completed.

Switch: A device used to break or open an electrical circuit, or to divert current from one conductor to another, that acts as a bridge for the current when closed.

T

Terminal: A device attached to the end of a conductor or to electrical apparatus for convenience in making electrical connections.

Tinning: The process of melting solder onto a conductor end to fuse individual strands into a solid wire.

Transformer: A device using mutual inductance to convert variations of an electrical current in a primary circuit into variations of current and voltage in a secondary circuit.

Transmission Lines: Any conductor or system of conductors used to carry electrical energy from its source to a secondary distribution system or to a load.

U

UF Cable: A type of cable sheathed in special plastic approved for use as underground feeder and branch circuit wiring, in wet, dry or corrosive locations, but not approved for burial in concrete or exposure to sunlight.

V

VA: Volt-ampere, a unit of electrical measurement equal to the product of a volt and an ampere that for direct current is the equivalent of a watt of power.

Volt: The mks unit of electrical force or potential difference, equal to the force needed to cause a current of 1 ampere to flow through a conductor resistance of 1 ohm.

Voltage Drop: Also called IR drop; a drop in the line voltage in the conductors of a circuit, caused by resistance or impedance.

Voltmeter: An instrument used to directly measure a difference in electrical potential, in volts.

W

Watt: The mks unit of power equal to the rate of work represented by a current of 1 ampere flowing through a conductor under a force of 1 volt.

Watt-hour Meter: An instrument used to measure electrical energy consumption over periods of time in kilowatt-hours; the electric meter that is a part of every residential (and other) electrical service.

Wattmeter: An instrument used to measure electrical power in watts.